The Garden Lover's Guide to the West

PRINCETON ARCHITECTURAL PRESS   NEW YORK

KATHLEEN MCCORMICK

The Garden Lover's Guide
to the West

Published by
Princeton Architectural Press
37 East 7th Street
New York, NY 10003
www.papress.com

© 2000 Princeton Architectural Press
ISBN 1-56898-166-x
04 03 02 01 00   5 4 3 2 1 First Edition
Printed and bound in China.

BOOK DESIGN: Adam Bohannon
COVER DESIGN: Sara E. Stemen
EDITING: Eugenia Bell

Special thanks to: Ann Alter, Amanda Atkins, Jan Cigliano, Jane Garvie,
Caroline Green, Beth Harrison, Mia Ihara, Clare Jacobson, Leslie Ann
Kent, Mark Lamster, Anne Nitschke, Lottchen Shivers, Jennifer Thompson,
and Deb Wood of Princeton Architectural Press
—Kevin C. Lippert, publisher

Library of Congress Cataloging-in-Publication Data
McCormick, Kathleen, 1955-
The garden lover's guide to the West / by Kathleen McCormick.— 1st ed.
p. cm. — (The garden lover's guides)
Includes index.
ISBN 1-56898-166-X (alk. paper)
1. Gardens—West (U.S.)—Guidebooks. 2. West (U.S.)—Guidebooks.
I. Title. II. Series.
SB466.U6 M37 2000
712'.0978—dc21   00-008109
                                                             CIP

Contents

This guide is written for travelers who wish to visit the most historic and beautiful gardens in the Western United States, from the formal estate gardens of California, to the unique xeriscapes of the deserts, and the lush, tropical gardens of the Hawaiian islands.

The book is divided into five chapters covering the major sites of the western states. Each chapter comprises an introductory section with a regional map and a list of the gardens, followed by entries on each garden. The numbers found on the regional maps can be used to locate the numbered entries within the chapters. These entries are accompanied by detailed at-a-glance information telling the reader about the garden's main characteristics and nearby sights of interest. The guide also includes six major gardens, beautifully illustrated with three-dimensional plans.

KEY TO SYMBOLS

Refreshments in vicinity	⛶
Formal garden	⛶
Landscape garden	⛶
House major feature	⛶
Historic garden	⛶
Kitchen garden	⛶
Botanic interest/rare plants	⛶
Topiary	⛶
Borders	⛶
Water features	⛶
Architectural features	⛶

Regional maps show
locations of gardens.

Each regional map includes a
numbered key to make finding
garden entries easy.

Entries begin with at-a-glance
information on opening times,
directions, nearby sights of
interest, and how to receive
further information.

Major gardens include watercolor
plans that note special features.

Introduction

One of my greatest pleasures is traveling to new places and learning about a region and its history and people through its gardens. For many years as I've hiked and bicycled through Ireland, the British Isles, Europe, Costa Rica, and North America, I've planned itineraries around pilgrimages to grand historic estates, parks, and botanic gardens—stopping frequently to admire gardens in front of private homes, pubs, and churches in every village. In both my professional life as a writer and my private life as a borderline-obsessive gardener, I've made it my mission to visit intriguing gardens, many of which appear in this book.

Having lived on the East Coast for most of my life, I moved to Colorado a few years ago, drawn by the beauty of the landscapes. With each subsequent year, my appreciation for Western gardens has deepened. Gardens of the Western states are among the most beautiful—often situated in spectacular natural settings—and the most varied of any region in the United States, with radically different climates, soils, and elevations. The 114 gardens in this book reflect the dramatically diverse backgrounds of their creators and benefactors—soldiers, settlers, missionaries; gold, lumber, and media barons; and garden designers and horticulturists who have joined artistry with a love of plants to create their own individual and regional garden styles.

What all these gardens have in common is a devotion to the creative forces of the garden, to endless hours of working the land, defying the elements, and catering to the predilections of plants themselves to express a vision of beauty. Gardens thrive or decline with the fortunes and whims of their creators and caretakers. Many of the finest gardens in this guide evolved into life-long labors of love, some like enduring marriages, surpassing half a century. Though perhaps not surprising, it is inspiring that many of these garden creators have lived and gardened well into their eighties and nineties. Their gift to all of us sharing their creative spirit is generous indeed.

MISSOULA 8

MOSCOW
13

MONTANA

BOISE
14

IDAHO

WYOMING

CHEYENNE
9

SALT LAKE CITY
10,11,12

FORT COLLINS 1

DENVER
5   2
         3,4

COLORADO SPRINGS
6,7

UTAH

COLORADO

1 Fort Collins: W.D.Holley Plant Environmental
   Research Center
2 Denver: Denver Botanic Gardens
3 Littleton: Chatfield Arboretum
4 Littleton: Hudson Gardens
5 Vail: Betty Ford Alpine Gardens
6 Colorado Springs: Horticultural Art Society
   Garden
7 Colorado Springs: Xeriscape Demonstration
   Garden

8 Missoula: Memorial Rose Garden
9 Cheyenne: Cheyenne Botanic Gardens
10 Salt Lake City: Red Butte Garden and Arboretum
11 Salt Lake City: International Peace Gardens
12 Salt Lake City: The Gardens at Temple Square
13 Moscow: University of Idaho Arboretum and
   Botanical Garden
14 Boise: Idaho Botanical Garden

ROCKY MOUNTAIN REGION

Colorado, Montana, Wyoming, Utah, Idaho

G iven the region's dry climate, intense sunlight and wind, summer hailstorms, and temperature extremes (ranging from below freezing to over 100 degrees), hardy, drought-tolerant plants that can thrive at high altitudes are most welcome here. Rocky Mountain gardens take their cue from the region's spectacular natural gardens displaying native wildflowers such as columbine and penstemons and trees including piñon pines and spruces. These gardens also feature plants from similar climates around the world. Spanish and Mexican traders and settlers brought herbs and crops from their homelands to New Mexico. Early pioneers from the East and Midwest created homestead gardens, and those who did well in the Gold Rush created Victorian gardens to go with their clapboard farmhouses or brick homes in the cities.

Today, the region's public gardens are popular places that appeal to both visitors and local gardeners seeking inspiration and suggestions for such challenges as drying winds and rocky and clay soils. The Denver Botanic Gardens' 23 acres are preeminent in this respect, with 30 distinct garden areas, from romantic borders of old-fashioned perennials to a rock-alpine garden with tough but tiny plants from mountain regions worldwide. The Chatfield Arboretum in Littleton displays water-conserving gardens and employs handsome trees and shrubs as windbreaks. The Xeriscape Demonstration Garden in Colorado Springs offers a compact, residential-style garden of drought-tolerant plants with a backdrop of red-rock mountains. In Vail, the Betty Ford Alpine Gardens—where wildflowers, perennials, roses,

OPPOSITE: *The view of Salt Lake City from the Red Butte Garden*

I

and evergreens embellish sandstone paths and waterfalls—prove that high-altitude gardening is its own reward.

Summertime brings blooms to parks, cottage gardens, and window boxes throughout the mountain towns, Plains communities, and cities of Wyoming, Montana, Utah, and Idaho. The hardiest of plants bloom in Missoula's Memorial Rose Garden and the Cheyenne Botanic Garden, both testaments to strong community support. In Boise, a former prison yard has been transformed by the Idaho Botanical Garden's heirloom roses, meditation garden, and butterfly garden. Sandstone formations inspired the name of Red Butte Garden in Salt Lake City, where terrace gardens of herbs, flowers, and cascading water are carved into a steep slope. In Salt Lake City, 35 countries from around the world celebrate their own garden styles and architecture at the International Peace Gardens.

The Rockies embrace the
Xeriscape Demonstration
Garden

Fort Collins: W.D.Holley Plant Environmental Research Center

LOCATION: ON THE COLORADO STATE UNIVERSITY CAMPUS, AT 630 WEST LAKE STREET

GARDEN OPEN: Dawn to dusk daily

ADMISSION: Free

FURTHER INFORMATION FROM: Department of Horticulture and Landscape Architecture Colorado State University 111 Shepardson Building Fort Collins 80523-1173. 970.491.7019

Though art and science are not mutually exclusive in the garden world, the W.D. Holley Plant Environmental Research Center celebrates their felicitous marriage. The beauty of this garden of flowers, vegetables, fruits, and hardy trees and shrubs belies the fact that it serves the aims of science. The garden was established in 1978 so CSU students, researchers, and the gardening public could observe plants in action. Its mission is to develop and maintain documented collections of woody and herbaceous plants, turf, and other botanic specimens appropriate to the Rocky Mountain and High Plains regions. It also aims to inspire stewardship of the environment and to promote the aesthetic aspects of garden design and planning. In this, the gardens provide an example of attractive layouts and demonstration gardens using plants appropriate for home gardens. The perennial garden beds brim with dozens of drought-hardy plants, including bee balm, lavender, desert four o'clocks, Russian sage, butterfly bush, black-eyed Susans (*Rudbeckia*), and ornamental grasses. Sections of the garden laid out by plant family include garden beds for the testing of new vegetable and annual flowers, herbs, woody plants, grapes and small fruits, and hedge plants that make good windbreaks and garden enclosures in this dry and often windy region. The adjacent arboretum covers 1,200 different taxa of trees and shrubs including maples, lindens, and viburnums. Regional favorites like crabapples—57 different cultivars—make this test garden especially lovely in spring.

Annual plots tended by CSU students and researchers at the W.D. Holley Plant Research Center

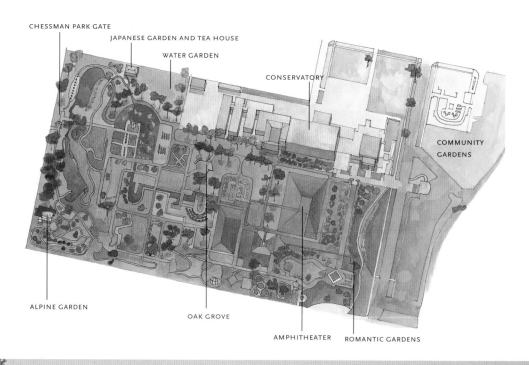

CHESSMAN PARK GATE

JAPANESE GARDEN AND TEA HOUSE

WATER GARDEN

CONSERVATORY

COMMUNITY GARDENS

ALPINE GARDEN

OAK GROVE

AMPHITHEATER

ROMANTIC GARDENS

2 Denver: Denver Botanic Gardens

LOCATION: EAST OF DOWNTOWN DENVER, BETWEEN YORK STREET AND
CHEESMAN PARK

Extending over 23 acres with 30 distinct garden areas ranging
from romantic perennial borders to the grasses and wildflowers
of the High Plains, the Denver Botanic Gardens comprise the
Rocky Mountain region's preeminent botanical collection. The
gardens have evolved over the past four decades from primarily
annual flowerbed displays to a broad array of gardens that celebrate special horticultural collections and handsomely designed
ornamental gardens. The gardens were founded in City Park
near the Denver Museum of Natural History in 1951 by the
newly formed Botanical Gardens Foundation of Denver. In
1959, the gardens moved to their present site on 18 acres of
open land owned by the city of Denver that had been occupied
by the (since relocated) Mt. Calvary Cemetery. The staff
assumed new offices in Waring House, a 1927 Norman-style
home on an adjacent parcel of land that was donated to the gardens. The renowned American landscape architect Garrett
Eckbo created the master plan for the gardens, and landscape
architects and garden designers of note, including Lauren
Springer, Herb Schall, Jane Silverstein Reis, and S.R. DeBoer,
designed many of the individual gardens. The Denver Parks
Department owns and continues to maintain the gardens, with
assistance from the foundation.

   Near the entrance and visitor center, the recently renovated Boettcher Memorial Conservatory invites visitors into the
rain forest. Designed by architect Victor Hornbein and dedicated in 1966, the modern, glass-and-concrete-domed conservatory now displays tropical plants on several levels accessible
by elevator in the 51-foot-high space. This ersatz rain forest is
much like the real thing: the air is dense and moist with
humidity from waterfalls, streams, pools, and misters—a quartet that spontaneously creates water music. Large leafy plants
such as banana trees and cycads (whose ancestors date back 50
million years) create a canopy over smaller flowering plants
such as red ginger lilies and Maui ixora with shiny dark leaves
and coral-colored blooms. Orchids and bromeliads fill the
attached Marnie's Pavilion.

   The East-West Path ushers visitors through the Colorado
Quartet Borders, including a "water-smart" garden with native
plants and adaptable exotics that thrive on low water and
intense sunshine. The path continues past a shaded woodland
to the Water Garden, where a temporary exhibit celebrates the
spirit of impressionist painter Claude Monet's gardens at
Giverny. The Water Garden features a lovely collection of large
pink, white, and red waterlilies hybridized by French horticulturist Joseph Bory Latour-Marliac. Beyond the Water Garden is

GARDEN OPEN: 9am–5pm
Wednesday–Friday,
9am–8pm Saturday–Tuesday,
May through September;
9am–5pm daily October
through April

ADMISSION: $5.50 adults,
$3.50 seniors, $3 students
and children 6-15, children
under 6 free

FURTHER INFORMATION FROM:
1005 York Street
Denver 80206.
303.331.4000

NEARBY SIGHTS OF INTEREST:
Denver Museum of Natural
History, Denver Zoo, Denver
Museum of Art, Denver
Public Library, Denver
Children's Museum

OPPOSITE: *Twin pavilions
define the architectural style
of the romantic Gardens*

TOP: *The Shofu'en Japanese garden*
BOTTOM: *The Boettcher Memorial Conservatory's rain forest*

the intimate and beautifully tended *Shofu-en*, or Garden of Pine Wind, designed in the late 1970s by Koichi Kawana, then professor of Japanese landscape design at the University of California, Los Angeles. In mile-high Denver, some of the plants are different than those found in Japanese gardens at lower elevations: wind-twisted Ponderosa pines and tough Asian maples are admirable stand-ins for their less-hardy Japanese cousins, and Korean lilacs, flowering plum, and crabapples substitute for azaleas and cherry trees. Water features such as a koi pond and a stream with banks of iris and thyme lend authentic symbolic details, as does the tea house, which was built in Japan and reassembled at the garden.

Continuing south, the Plains garden—a naturalized area that mixes various native grasses and wildflowers such as big bluestem, Mexican hat, evening primrose, blanket flower, and prairie flax—gives a wide-open feel in a relatively small space. The southwest corner of the garden, with views of Mt. Evans to the west, is my favorite spot: the Rock-Alpine Garden, recognized as perhaps the premiere example of rock gardening in North America. Fashioned from 500 tons of five kinds of rock that create slopes and berms, this single acre is intensively planted with a quarter of the botanic gardens' entire collection of plants. Designed by landscape architect Herb Schaal of EDAW, Inc., the garden is both an ornamental rock garden and a regional plant experimentation station, where plants from alpine regions around the world are tested for their adaptability to the Rocky Mountain region. The garden displays intricate layering of many tiny, tough, mat-like alpine plants with bulbs, succulents, small shrubs—ranging from Himalayan rock jasmine to ice plants from South Africa. The garden's plantings reflect the horticultural expertise of Panayoti Kelaidis, DBG's curator of plant collections and a plant explorer who propagates wild-collected seed from far-flung regions such as Patagonia and Central Asia. Kelaidis especially loves iconoclastic color combinations, such as tiny magenta tulips popping up amid sulfur-yellow-flowering *Draba siberica* with apple-green foliage.

A fountain to the east of the alpine garden leads into the Wingsong Garden of small trees and shrubs with berries that attract birds. Returning north toward the center of the garden, you'll encounter the May Bonfils-Stanton Rose Garden, where old-fashioned shrub roses mingle with other heirloom flowers like foxglove, lamb's ear, and lavender, and standard miniature roses consort with colorful and fragrant annuals. Heading south, you'll find a peony garden, and beyond it a home demonstration garden with a gazebo surrounded by trees, flowering perennials and bulbs, a pool and waterfall, and low-maintenance ground covers. Also along the south side is an herb garden with brick paths that encircle beds of culinary, medicinal, and dye plants and the 1898 statue *The Boy and a Frog* by Denver sculptor Elsie Ward Hering. Next to it is the Scripture Garden, created by Denver landscape architect Jane Silverstein Ries. One of the smallest gardens, it is also one of its most intriguing, with plants mentioned in the Bible, a reflecting pool, and benches that invite contemplation. Plants in this garden that are not winter-hardy like palms, pomegranates, and figs spend the cold months in the gardens' greenhouses.

In the southeast corner, the Romantic Gardens hold sway with serpentine brick paths, a central lawn and perennial beds, pavilions, a plaza and courtyard, water features, and a long luxurious perennial walk. The Romantic Gardens are meant to stimulate the senses and evoke a sense of ideal harmony with the world. Designed as a series of five "rooms," each offers distinctive plantings and architectural details: the largest room features aromatic plants in pastel pinks and blues, with details such as an arts-and-crafts-style tulip design incorporated in metal fence panels, garden arbors, and lattice fencing. The El Pomar Waterway, a long narrow canal modeled on the creations of noted Mexican architect Luis Barragán, uses ceramic tile, stucco walls, and a sheeting waterfall to create a sense of fantasy and exotic locale. A wide path of soft, unmortared brick promenades through the perennial walk's deep borders of plants arranged in a symphony of colors and textures. Designed by horticulturist Lauren Springer and Denver Botanic Garden Director Rob Proctor, the plantings flow in alternating color blocks, with rapturous combinations such as tall mauve Joe Pye weed, purple coneflower, Russian sage, sea lavender, lilies, roses, and snapdragons. By the time you have reached the cooler whites and yellows at the end of the walk, which returns to the entrance, you're pleasantly saturated in a world of the senses.

ABOVE: *Prairie grasses are the signature plants of the Laura Porter Smith Plains Garden*
BELOW: *Water lily pool near the Monet Garden*

GARDEN OPEN: 9am–5pm
daily except holidays in winter
ADMISSION: $1 adults, chil-
dren under 16 free
FURTHER INFORMATION FROM:
8500 Deer Creek Canyon
Road
Littleton 80128.
303.973.3705
NEARBY SIGHTS OF INTEREST:
Hudson Gardens, South
Platte River hike and bike trail

3 Littleton: Chatfield Arboretum

LOCATION: SOUTHWEST OF DOWNTOWN DENVER, NEAR WADSWORTH BOULE-
VARD AND ROUTE 470 INTERSECTION

Located southwest of Denver near the Rocky Mountain
foothills, the Chatfield Arboretum covers 700 acres of
woodlands, wetlands, farmland, and gardens steeped in
Colorado history. For wildlife enthusiasts, this landscape
offers many attractions: Deer, elk, coyote, and porcupine
live in the groves, and numerous species of birds such as
Western meadowlarks, great blue herons, American
kestrels, and the great horned owl make their home here. In
addition to displaying native trees, flowers, and wildlife, the
site hosts two nineteenth-century farms and a one-room
schoolhouse. In 1866, Frank Hildebrand homesteaded the
site. The land remained in his family until the mid-1970s,
when the U.S. Army Corps of Engineers built the Chatfield
Reservoir, and it became a flood plain. The arboretum is
leased from the U.S. Army Corps of Engineers and managed by the Denver Botanic Gardens. The historic farm-
house and its outbuildings are on the National Register of
Historic Places. Farm buildings have been renovated for use
as administrative offices, a classroom, and a maintenance
shop, with a nature center in the old bunkhouse. The
restored 1870s Deer Creek School, formerly located down-
stream from the farms, was moved here to higher ground
and is used as a visitor center. Around these buildings are
gardens of dryland perennials designed by Boulder landscape architect Jim Knopf and local horticulturist Marcia
Tatroe. In both gardens, water-wise plants that attract butterflies, bees, and birds, including sages, penstemons, butterfly weed, pasque flower, and columbines, are nestled
among rocks and native grasses. After a century of farming,
the grasslands have been re-seeded with more than a dozen
native species. The arboretum's mission, in fact, is to showcase plants of the region, and particularly of the prairie and
foothills. Two miles of trails provide a closer look at many of
these plants. The Dora & Pauline Roberts riparian trail follows Deer Creek and connects to trails around the wetland
ponds. A survival garden displays plants of the West that
traditionally have been used for food and medicine by
Native Americans and early settlers. A tree-walk booklet
identifies mountain alders, Ponderosa pines, bluestem willows, red hawthorns, and other native trees. The arboretum
has also planted 90 species of drought-resistant trees and
shrubs as windbreaks and to aid in research on which trees
adapt best to the Front Range's arid climate and dramatically fluctuating temperatures. Plant lists and self-guided
tour materials help visitors learn about the plants, wildlife,

OPPOSITE: *A butterfly-
shaped garden features perennials and ornamental grasses
with the Hudson's house in
the background*

and history of the site. The arboretum's biggest event of the year, the Pumpkin Festival, usually held the first week of October, draws thousands of families to its pumpkin patches.

4 Littleton: Hudson Gardens

LOCATION: SOUTHWEST OF DOWNTOWN DENVER, AT 6115 SOUTH SANTE FE DRIVE

Opened in June 1996, Hudson Gardens was begun decades earlier as the dream of the late Evelyn Hudson. In 1941, Evelyn and her husband, Colonel King C. Hudson, purchased a parcel of land on the South Platte River, south of Denver, that boasted spectacular views of the Rocky Mountains. They built a log-cabin style restaurant that gained national acclaim. During the next 20 years, they added to the property and cared for it with an environmental consciousness unusual in that era. Before she died in 1988, Evelyn established the Hudson Foundation to protect the property from commercial development. Through grants,

Garden open: 10am–5pm daily, weather permitting
ADMISSION: $4 adults, $3 seniors, $2 children ages 6-12, children under 6 free
FURTHER INFORMATION FROM: 2888 West Maplewood Avenue
Littleton 80120-1807.
303.797.8565
NEARBY SIGHTS OF INTEREST: South Platte River hike and bike trail

donations, and community volunteer efforts, as well as an alliance with the South Suburban Park and Recreation District, the gardens claim a mission as a regional display garden to provide education and pleasure. The 30 acres of gardens comprise 16 distinctive gardens that display trees, shrubs, and flowers that flourish in the region's dry climate. Landscape architect Doug Rockne and master horticulturist Andrew Pierce laid out the gardens as a series of "rooms with a view," each flowing into the next. The sweet, pungent, and spicy fragrances of old-fashioned roses, lilacs, and herbs such as lavender, fennel, and rosemary waft down from the fragrance garden that crowns a cobblestone retaining wall. The oval garden of lawn with an enormous butterfly-shaped perennial border features massings of plants with lots of texture and long-term color, such as veronica, yarrow, gallardia, butterfly bush, and ornamental grasses. To the west of it is the historical rose garden, whose pergolas and fountain direct the eye to views of snow-capped peaks. Contained within a perimeter of dwarf privet are hybrid teas, musks, and rugosas mingling with other old blooms introduced as early as the mid-1800s. In the cutting garden east of the Hudson's dusty pink ranch house, sea lavender, purple cone-flower, and coreopsis are offset by red buds, glossy buck-thorn, and blue spruces planted half a century ago by King Hudson. One of Hudson's most charming gardens embraces the front of the house—an English-style cottage garden, designed by horticulturist Lauren Springer. The riot of tex-tures and colors include giant kale, ornamental alliums, spiky penstemons, and foxgloves. On a slope behind the house are a butterfly garden and demonstration beds (a café offers snacks for garden visitors and travelers along the hike and bike trail that runs between the gardens and the South Platte River). A wetlands formed by a flood in 1965 has been transformed into a water garden with sweet flag, iris, and water lilies. Wooden benches set beneath huge cottonwoods provide a perfect spot to drink in the views. Over the bridge, a winding path leads past a wildflower meadow to the secret garden, a delight for children with its wide timber swing peeking through a screen of mock orange and dogwood. Further east, a rocky cascade garden and two acres of conifer groves provide a habitat for birds. Across the bowl-shaped lawn (an amphitheater for summer concerts) is the rock gar-den, where tiny alpine plants bloom in the hot dry gravel next to tall white balloon flowers.

5 Vail: Betty Ford Alpine Gardens

LOCATION: IN GERALD R. FORD PARK, OFF SOUTH FRONTAGE ROAD OF I-70
EAST BETWEEN VAIL VILLAGE AND EAST VAIL

GARDEN OPEN: Dawn to dusk, snowmelt to snowfall

ADMISSION: Free

FURTHER INFORMATION FROM:
Vail Alpine Garden
Foundation
18 Gore Creek Drive
Vail 81657.
970.476.0103

The gardening season is short at an elevation of 8,200 feet, but the Betty Ford Alpine Gardens make the most of it in all their ephemeral glory. Nestled on a slope next to the Gore Creek in Gerald R. Ford Park, the two-acre botanical garden is a showcase for alpine perennials, shrubs, and trees that thrive at this altitude. In fact, the plants seem to grow almost supernaturally well, in part because the thin mountain air and intense sunlight seem to super-saturate colors. In these gardens, foliage of a dozen rich greens from chartreuse to spruce provide a background for the deep periwinkle of Rocky Mountain columbines, the rich pinks and purples of lupines, and the radiant yellows of alpine daisies and ice plants. In the mid-1980s, the Vail Alpine Garden Foundation, a small group of Vail and Denver horticulturists, began working to create a garden that would cultivate harmony between plants and people in the region. In 1988, the gardens were named in honor of Betty Ford, wife of President Gerald R. Ford, for her contributions to the Vail Valley. One of the highest public gardens in North America, it is used for teaching environmentally sensitive gardening techniques appropriate for the region's fragile ecosystems and its extreme conditions of high-altitude, low moisture, variations in temperature, and intense sunlight. Local buff-colored sandstone steps and paths lead through four sections representing different perspectives on the Rocky Mountains. The alpine display garden near the entrance features 500 different alpine and sub-alpine plants in four microclimates and also incorporates dryland plants, a cliff garden, a peat bed, and a woodland area. The mountain perennial garden displays another 1,500 varieties, such as alpine poppies, penstemons, veronicas, primrose, and vibrant trumpet gentians gathered around a waterfall and pond. The focus of the mountain meditation garden, in the Eastern tradition, is rock and water—a pool and stream surrounded by conifers, kinnikinick, iris, and a carpet of thyme. The dappled shade, the water music, and the textures in this garden make it a tranquil place. The new alpine rock garden at the highest point of the ravine will feature rock-alpine plants from North America and around the world. Covered with snow much of the year, the gardens emerge in a kaleidoscope of color when the snow does melt (usually in May). In this resort town, the gardens draw many summer visitors to marvel over their quilt of wildflowers and other alpine blooms that peak about a month later than in Denver and two months later than at sea level.

A rich tapestry of multi-colored foliage graces the natural settings at the Alpine Gardens

6 # Colorado Springs: Horticultural Art Society Garden

GARDEN OPEN: Sunrise to
sunset daily

ADMISSION: Free

FURTHER INFORMATION FROM:
Horticultural Art Society of
Colorado Springs
PO Box 7706
Colorado Springs 80933-
7706.

NEARBY SIGHTS OF INTEREST:
Cheyenne Mountain Zoo,
Xeriscape Demonstration
Garden, Fine Arts Center
Sculpture Garden

LOCATION: UINTAH STREET EXIT OF I-25, IN MONUMENT VALLEY PARK, AT COR-
NER OF MESA ROAD AND GLEN AVENUE

The Horticultural Art Society of Colorado Springs is a group of
gardeners dedicated to learning about plants that grow well in
the high, dry Pikes Peak region. Judging from the society's
demonstration garden in Monument Valley Park, its members
have green thumbs and artistic palettes. Tucked in between
Monument Creek and the railroad tracks next to Interstate 25,
the garden graces a spot that easily could have been left a wasteland. But it charms with a quiet, old-fashioned beauty, as
though the flowers and herbs, rocks and woodlands were
plucked from an Impressionist painting. The garden was
started in 1962, when the City of Colorado Springs offered the
land at the corner of Mesa and Glen, where large blue spruce
and white fir trees dated to the turn of the century, along with
venerable plains cottonwoods, elms, and oaks. Volunteers from
local garden clubs donated time, materials, and ornamental
items. These gardeners evolved into the Horticultural Art
Society, which continues to plant and maintain the garden.

Old-fashioned perennials
paint a charming canvas

Nearly 40 years later, the demonstration garden displays a regional garden style that features traditional perennial plantings as well as plants of the Rocky Mountains, the High Plains, and the Southwest. The centerpiece of the garden is a 1732 marble fountain from Pisa, Italy, surrounded by cream-colored Meideland roses and taller, pink David Austin roses. North and south of the fountain are beds of annuals and perennials, including peonies, phlox, dahlias, black-eyed Susans, and anemones. Further north, a fragrance garden of herbs and flowers with interesting smells and textures such as lavender, sage, and petunias pleases the senses, and is designed with handicapped visitors in mind. A children's garden delights with sunflowers, strawberries, and a teepee of climbing gourds. Crevices in the rock garden are filled with columbine, while a stream in the woodland garden trickles past asters, cardinal flower, ninebark, and other mountain plants. Beds carved into the lawn display All-American selections of annuals and vegetables. Further north in the park, beyond the cottage and city greenhouse, are the willow pond, a rose garden, and a heritage garden with a 1914 Van Briggle sun clock. Though spanning less than an acre, these gardens are inspired compositions that could fill the most admired canvases.

7 Colorado Springs: Xeriscape Demonstration Garden

LOCATION: IN NORTHWEST COLORADO SPRINGS, AT THE CITY'S WATER RESOURCES DEPARTMENT FACILITY ON MESA ROAD

GARDEN OPEN: Dawn to dusk daily

ADMISSION: Free

FURTHER INFORMATION FROM: Water Resources Department 2855 Mesa Road Colorado Springs 80904–1199. 719.448.4555 www.csu.org/xeri

At first glance, it might seem that the allure of the Colorado Springs Utilities' Xeriscape Demonstration Garden is the borrowed scenery of Pike's Peak and the red-rock formations of the Garden of the Gods. The uninterrupted views of meadows and mountains are truly magnificent, but the garden itself is also captivating, if in a more subtle way. In just under an acre, this garden displays more than 70 native plants and 400 species, including dozens of different penstemons, those spiky plants with tubular pink, red, and blue flowers that hummingbirds love so much. Serpentine sandstone paths wind through four water zones of plants that require very little to no irrigation. The original garden, begun in the 1970s, was transformed in the early 1990s into a xeriscape garden, as that concept of hydro-zoning to conserve water became popular in the region. Today, the former parking lot is packed with xeric (from the Greek for "dry") plants with beautiful colors and textures and hardy habits, arranged in a design that could be any gardener's

front yard. In a very low water area, ground covers such as yellow and purple-flowering ice plant rim beds with flowers like orange butterfly weed and shrubs such as Persian lilac, woods rose, and rock spirea. A rock garden offers scarlet cup and prickly pear cactus, while a stone path is softened with spreading thyme. Japanese blood grass and other ornamental grasses bank a berm, and golden buffalo grass cuts swaths in the place of a thirstier bluegrass lawn. After strolling this complex little garden one hot summer afternoon, my daughter and I found a cool spot beneath a trellis draped with clematis to contemplate the views. The garden in the foreground and the mountains beyond came into focus together to compose an awe-inspiring view.

8 Missoula: Memorial Rose Garden

LOCATION: 700 BROOK STREET

Missoula is known as "The Garden City" in Montana, and the city blooms in summer with lots of home gardens and annual flower beds in city parks and public places. The Memorial Rose Garden, an All-American Rose Selections display garden with more than 1,000 rose bushes, is a special testament to the care, skill, and tenacity of the gardeners who created and maintain it—not to mention the plants themselves, given Missoula's long cold winters that test even the hardiest of plants. The garden was started in 1944 by the Missoula Rose Society, which spent two years fundraising for a site and planning a memorial garden for Montana's casualties of World War II. In 1946, the society planted the first beds around a memorial obelisk with 630 rose bushes. In 1947, the garden became an American Rose Society test garden, and eventually it became one of 130 All-American Rose Selections gardens, which display new varieties chosen for their beauty, novelty, and vigor. The society cares for the garden in a joint agreement with the Missoula Parks Department. Spanning two blocks in an older residential neighborhood, the garden is laid out with beds and grass paths arranged in a rectangle around the central obelisk. At the north end are paved pathways leading to newer memorials, including a bronze angel holding a soldier, a memorial to those killed in Vietnam, and a black granite memorial to those who fought the Korean War. Old species roses are scattered throughout the garden, which was restored in 1989 and again in 1995 after vandals cut down many of the bushes. The beds are organized by winners for each year. Shrub roses—including the Kaleidoscope, whose color changes from mauve to dusty rose—bloom along the outer perimeter, then floribundas and grandifloras, with hybrid teas gathered around the obelisk. Four arbors leading

ABOVE: A typically breathtaking view from the Xeriscape Demonstration Garden

into these main beds are draped with clematis and climbing roses, especially challenging to grow because of the deep winter freezes. Given the magnificent views of the mountains that surround the Bitterroot Valley and the shade of large maples, oaks, and pines, the garden is a beautiful place for meditation, though it is also enjoyed by picnickers, Frisbee players, and by children using the small playground at the north end.

9 Cheyenne: Cheyenne Botanic Gardens

LOCATION: WITHIN LIONS PARK

GARDEN OPEN 8am–4:30pm weekdays, 11am–3:30pm weekends and most holidays
ADMISSION: Free
FURTHER INFORMATION FROM:
710 S. Lions Park Drive
Cheyenne, WY 82001.
307.637.6458
www.botanic.org
NEARBY SIGHTS OF INTEREST:
Old West Museum, Sloans Lake

The Cheyenne Botanic Gardens is famous for its sustainability, both in terms of the environment and in its support from the community. Wyoming's tough climate presents certain challenges for a botanic garden: It leads the nation in number of annual hail storms, comes in fourth for wind, and has wildly fluctuating temperatures, falling to well below zero degrees Fahrenheit and spiking above 100. At an elevation of over 6,000 feet, Cheyenne has cool nights even in summer (an 80-day tomato takes 120 days to ripen). Until recent decades, the city was basically a treeless plain; in 1867, in fact, the city had only 12 trees. Fortunately, this high-desert community has plenty of sunny days and people committed to their botanic garden, which is housed in a model energy-conserving green-

The solar-heated and solar-powered conservatory

house. Opened in 1977 as a private nonprofit venture, the Community Solar Greenhouse was intended for seniors, youth, and handicapped clients to grow plants and vegetables year-round. In 1986, the greenhouse was moved to its present site in Lions Park and became part of the Cheyenne Parks and Recreation Department. Today, the 6,800 square-foot green-house conservatory, 100-percent solar-heated and 30-percent solar-powered, receives support from a foundation and many volunteers, most of whom are seniors, children, disabled, or "at risk" youth. The conservatory consists of three greenhouses: the east greenhouse grows some 50,000 flowering plants each year for the city parks. The west greenhouse features vegetables, and the center greenhouse has tropical plants such as citrus and banana trees, an herb garden, a waterfall, and a pond filled with koi. Outside the conservatory are four acres of designed gardens, with two more acres under construction. There are areas devoted to perennials, annuals, wildflowers, roses, a lily pond, a sensory garden, a cactus garden, and a peace garden. A walkway that connects the botanic garden with the Old West Museum features a xeriscape garden, a cottonwood grove, and a pond. This pathway eventually will have plazas, a dwarf conifer garden, a healing garden, and a children's garden.

10 **Salt Lake City: Red Butte Garden and Arboretum**

LOCATION: EAST OF THE UNIVERSITY OF UTAH'S RESEARCH PARK, AT 300 WAKARA WAY

GARDEN OPEN: 9am–8pm Monday–Saturday from May 1 through September 30, 10am–5pm Sundays and Tuesday–Sunday from October 1 through April 30 Admission: $5 adults, $3 seniors and children ages 4-15, children under 4 free

FURTHER INFORMATION FROM: RBG Administrative Offices 18A de Trobriand Street Salt Lake City 84113-5044. 801.581.4747 www.redbutte.utah.edu

NEARBY SIGHTS OF INTEREST: University of Utah campus, historic Fort Douglas

Tucked among the eastern foothills of the Salt Lake Valley, adjacent to the University of Utah campus, the nonprofit Red Butte Garden is the largest botanical and ecological center in the Intermountain West that tests, displays, and interprets regional horticulture. Red Butte stretches over 150 acres with walking paths and natural areas for hiking trails, as well as exhibits of trees, shrubs, and flowers. A partner in the Missouri-based Center for Plant Conservation, a national network of plant research and conservation institutions, the garden is home to 17 species of endangered native plants. Red Butte Garden also features a 1,500-acre arboretum with more than 9,000 specimens of trees and shrubs from around the world. The arboretum collection dates to 1931, when University of Utah botany professor Walter P. Cottam initiated decades of tree planting on the university campus, which led to the campus' designation in 1961 as the state arboretum. In 1983, the University of Utah dedicated 150 acres at the mouth of Red Butte Canyon for a regional botanical garden. The entrance into the garden, known as the Four Seasons Garden, invites visitors to enjoy grand views and the year-round kaleidoscope of winter's evergreens, spring's bulbs and flowering cherries and magnolias, summer's perennial flowers, and fall's foliage and fruits. A floral walk leads to the terrace gardens, separated into areas for herbs, medicinal plants, and plants with unusual fragrances. Carved into a steep slope, these gardens are designed as a series of descending terraces with walls of local red sandstone. Wisteria arbors lead to overlooks of lower gardens. On the upper terrace, an herb garden features boxwood parterres filled with traditional culinary plants and shrub roses. In the center is the medicinal herb garden, displaying plants used in research conducted at the university. The floral walk continues to a waterfall garden with day lilies, iris, and other perennials. A cascade tumbles from a water pavilion garden above containing water lilies and ornamental grasses. Beyond the butterfly-filled wildflower meadow is a natural area with four miles of trails leading through rugged terrain to ridges and canyons with views of the valley and Salt Lake City. One of the more unusual gardens is the new 1.5-acre children's garden, constructed with 300 tons of sandstone and 50 tons of boulders. A "sprout house" in the heart of the children's garden is a miniature working greenhouse with small-scale potting benches, tools, and classroom facilities. The children's garden also includes an adventure area with fountains, a 150-foot rattlesnake maze made from shrubs trained into tunnels, and an exploratory garden that teaches about ethnobotany.

The waterfall along Red Butte's floral walk

GARDEN OPEN: Dawn to dusk
daily from May through
October

ADMISSION: Free

FURTHER INFORMATION FROM:
1060 South, 900 West
Salt Lake City 84105.
801.974.2411

NEARBY SIGHTS OF INTEREST:
Gardens at Temple Square,
Red Butte Garden and
Arboretum

11 Salt Lake City: International Peace Gardens

LOCATION: WITHIN JORDAN PARK

Located on seven acres within Salt Lake's Jordan Park, with the Jordan River running through it, the International Peace Garden celebrates the gardens and cultures of all the city's ethnic groups. In the 1930s, the Salt Lake Council of Women created the garden to welcome immigrants from countries as far flung as Japan and Sweden. Their intent was to provide a way for various ethnic groups to celebrate the centennial of the state and have their own little piece of home in the city. Most of the immigrants had come to America five to ten years before, and the garden was a special place. The Peace Gardens lay dormant during World War II for lack of funds and volunteers. By the late 1940s, however, new gardens were being cultivated, and the international language of gardening was once again spoken fluently. Gardens representing 26 different countries now display their flags, commonly cultivated plants, and design elements that symbolize their history and culture. Visitors can meander through England's rose garden, past Denmark's replica of the Little Mermaid, to a miniature Matterhorn and chalet in the Swiss garden. Among the more recent additions are gardens representing Ethiopia and Tonga. The garden's greenhouse grows hundreds of varieties of exotic plants in 25 perennial beds and 50 annual beds. The garden is open from May through October, but because it's located at a relatively high elevation, it peaks from July through September, after the region warms up and before the fall's first frost. Though located in a public park, the garden is somewhat off the beaten path, which lends it a certain charm. It's a quiet place for reflection, and that's why people come.

GARDENS OPEN: 7am–10pm
daily

ADMISSION: Free

TOURS: Offered free several
times a day from April
through September.

FURTHER INFORMATION FROM:
The Church of Jesus Christ of
Latter-day Saints
15 East S. Temple Street
Salt Lake City 84111.
801.240.5916

12 Salt Lake City: The Gardens at Temple Square

LOCATION: AT TEMPLE SQUARE IN DOWNTOWN SALT LAKE CITY

The three city blocks of the Gardens at Temple Square, the headquarters of the Church of Jesus Christ of Latter-day Saints, are intended to show how Mother Nature would plant flowers: naturalized groupings and no straight lines unless it's a hedge. Geometry does play a part in the squares and circles containing planting beds and fountains, and the straight lines of pathways and allées of trees. Beginning in 1890 the church created the original gardens around its new temple to encourage peaceful contemplation. Today gardens and parkland cover 35 acres with flowering trees and more than 500 varieties of annuals and perennials. The design of each planting bed is different, with garden styles ranging from formal parterres to a nineteenth - century cottage garden surrounding the former home of Mormon leader and first governor of Utah, Brigham Young. Volunteers plant the beds twice each year with thousands of spring flowering bulbs such as tulips, hyacinths, and pansies and then with summer lilies, ornamental grasses, and annuals that continue blooming with chrysanthemums in the fall. A new rooftop prairie garden with waterways, located one block east of Temple Square, recently expanded the garden. Because planting depth can be no greater than 18 inches, and the mater-ial must be lightweight, a special mix of peat moss, utelite, and fertilizer is the planting medium for the rooftop beds. The gar-dens offer brilliant color and natural beauty amid the concrete glass, and metal of downtown Salt Lake City. An especially pop-ular time is the month of December, when thousands of lights are arrayed in the garden.

13 Moscow: University of Idaho Arboretum and Botanical Garden

LOCATION: EAST OF THE UNIVERSITY GOLF COURSE, BETWEEN NEZ PERCE DRIVE AND WEST PALOUSE RIVER DRIVE

GARDEN OPEN: Dawn to dusk daily

ADMISSION: Free

FURTHER INFORMATION FROM:
Arboretum Director
109-10 Alumni Center
University of Idaho
Moscow 83844-3226.
208.885.6250

Moscow was treeless until a century ago, when a University of Idaho forestry professor named Charles Houston Shattuck cre-ated the university's first arboretum on the barren slope south of the campus's administration building. From 1910–1917, Shattuck and forestry technician C.L. Price transformed the slope by planting many trees, including giant sequoias, incense cedars, Canadian hemlock, and Eastern American beeches. Two years after Shattuck's death in 1931, the university's Board of Regents named the arboretum after its founder. Today, the 14-acre Shattuck Arboretum continues to be a popular place for a peaceful walk. In 1975, the university put aside 63 acres one block south of the arboretum to construct a neighboring arboretum and botanic garden. Local volunteers constructed roads, ponds, and pipelines and hand-planted trees and shrubs. Since planting its first Asian crabapples in 1982, the garden has grown to encompass four major geographic collections—Asian, Eastern North American, Western North American, and European—sited around two ponds. Paths wind their way through groves of crabapples, ornamental cherries and pears, and shrub peonies in the Asian section. Among other Asian plants are many wild-collected specimens planted from seeds, including lilacs, viburnums, buckthorns, and vines. The

View of the botanical garden's two major ponds with flowering crabapples in the foreground

OPPOSITE: *The path leading to one of the Idaho Botanical Garden's sandstone buildings*

Western North American collection includes Alaska yellow cedars, native conifers, and several cultivars of Colorado spruce. The Eastern North American section showcases 13 species of oaks, and sugar, black, and red maples. In the European section, London plane trees mix with mountain ash, weeping larch, lindens, horse chestnuts, Scots pine, and Norway spruce. Throughout the collections, roses and shrubs such as mock-orange add fragrance and color. Granite benches sited at viewpoints invite visitors to ponder the many layers of color and texture, especially during spring blooms of lilacs and fruit trees and fall's burst of scarlet and golden hues. The arboretum and botanic garden will eventually include 11 acres of display gardens at the southern end, near a century-old barn that was part of a farm given to the university. Brochures and maps of the garden are available at the kiosk located in the northern end of the garden, which is surrounded by spring-flowering narcissus, snowdrops, and anemones, as well as barberries and junipers.

14 Boise: Idaho Botanical Garden

LOCATION: OFF WARM SPRINGS AVENUE, ON OLD PENITENTIARY ROAD

The high stone walls and guard towers of the Historic Idaho Prison adjacent to the Idaho Botanical Garden provide clues to the history of one of the garden world's more unusual sites. Opened in 1984 as a private, nonprofit institution on 50 acres leased from the state, the garden covers ground that once was the farm and nursery for the Idaho State Penitentiary. The old prison shut its gates in 1973 and for 12 years lay neglected until the botanical garden began to transform rock, weeds, and rubble into the gardens we see today. The buildings that prisoners constructed with sandstone they quarried from nearby Table Rock are open for public tours. Thirteen specialty gardens now cover ten acres. The heirloom rose garden flourishes against a guard tower, and the "outlaw field," where prisoners used to play baseball, is now an event lawn rimmed with ornamental grasses. The meditation garden was formerly the plant nursery, and trees planted here in the 1950s by minimum-security prisoners have grown tall enough to provide shady spots for contemplation next to the garden's stream. The Muriel and Diane Kirk English Garden, designed by renowned English landscape designer John Brooks, features roses, perennial flowers, and a fountain dedicated to Princess Diana. Other garden areas are devoted to herbs, peonies, cacti, native plants, water plants, an alpine trough garden, and a children's garden with raised vegetable beds and an alphabet area with plants representing each letter. The gardens are especially child-friendly and are used extensively for school groups studying botany and wildlife in settings such as the butterfly/hummingbird garden, where warm-hued annuals and perennials attract tiger swallowtail butterflies and black-chinned hummingbirds. An historical collection of iris—Dyke's medal-winning varieties from the 1920s—has been relocated to a new area of the garden. Situated on a hill, the garden offers magnificent sunsets, which visitors can enjoy while picnicking on summer nights (the garden is open on Thursdays in July and August until 9pm for Great Garden Escape programs of live music). Other community and family events include the Mad Hatter's Party in September and the Winter Garden Aglow festival in December, when the entire garden is illuminated.

GARDEN OPEN: 9am–5pm Monday–Thursday, 9am–8pm Friday, 10am–6pm Saturday and Sunday (April through October), 12–4pm winter

ADMISSION: $3 adults, $2 students, children under 6 free

FURTHER INFORMATION FROM: 2355 North Penitentiary Road P.O. Box 2140-83701 Boise 83712. 208.343.8649 www.idahobotanicalgarden.org

NEARBY SIGHTS OF INTEREST: Downtown Boise, Discovery Center of Idaho, Boise Tour Train

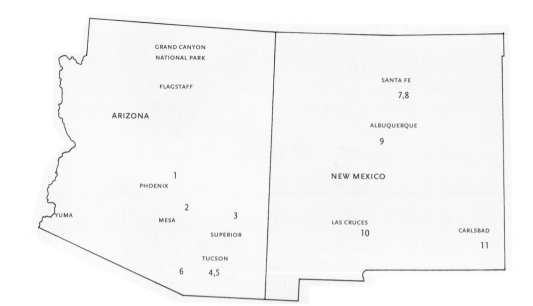

GRAND CANYON
NATIONAL PARK

FLAGSTAFF

ARIZONA

SANTA FE
7,8

ALBUQUERQUE
9

1
PHOENIX

NEW MEXICO

2
MESA

3

YUMA

SUPERIOR

LAS CRUCES
10

CARLSBAD
11

TUCSON

6   4,5

1 Phoenix: Desert Botanical Garden
2 Mesa: Mormon Temple Gardens
3 Superior: Boyce Thompson
   Arboretum
4 Tucson: Tohono Chul Park
5 Tucson: Tucson Botanical Gardens
6 Tucson: Arizona-Sonora Desert
   Museum
7 Santa Fe: Garden at El Zaguán
   (Bandelier Garden)
8 Santa Fe: El Rancho de las
   Golondrinas
9 Albuquerque: Rio Grande Botanical
   Garden
10 Las Cruces: New Mexico State
   University Landscape
   Demonstration Garden
11 Carlsbad: Living Desert Zoo &
   Gardens State Park

SOUTHWEST

Arizona, New Mexico

G iven the Southwest's climate—dry to parched, with wide variations in temperature from freezing nights to searing 120-degree days—it's no wonder that the region's gardens are all about dry-land plants. Given harsh conditions, plants such as cacti, agaves, and aloes prove that form follows function. Covered with sharp spines that protect them from animals, cacti store considerable reserves of water that allow them to live for months without rain. Fortunately for garden lovers, the desert has given birth to many of our toughest, most fascinating plants. The tall spikes of cream-colored blooms on agaves, the twisted limbs of junipers, and the barbed wands of the ocotillo with crowns of blood-red flowers can make a plain adobe wall a work of art. In these Southwest gardens, cooling tiled fountains, shade from the silvery-green palo verdes, and swaths of brilliant poppies and other wildflowers create splendid oases in the desert.

Whether tucked into a city neighborhood like the historic Tucson Botanical Gardens, or spread out over a mountainside with desert views for many miles like the Arizona-Sonora Desert Museum, the gardens of Arizona proudly feature the huge saguaro cactus, the state flower. With arms raised in salute, these sentries from the Sonoran Desert—the only place on earth where they grow in the wild— hold up to 5,000 gallons of water, live 75 years or more, and provide nesting spots for birds who burrow into their tough skin.

Their fruit was a primary source of food for the ancient Tohono O'odam Indians (also called the Papago), who held

OPPOSITE: *Potted succulents against a colorful adobe wall at the Arizona-Sonora Desert Museum*

23

the saguaro in such high esteem that they dated their calendar from the beginning of the saguaro harvest. Ethnobotanical gardens at the Desert Botanical Garden in Phoenix show how the Papago used the saguaro and other desert plants for food, fiber, and shelter.

Along the Rio Grande River in Albuquerque, New Mexico, a botanical garden that bears the river's name traces the flow of water from the mountains to the ocean, past rock formations that echo bluffs and mesas and plant communities of piñon pine and rabbitbrush, to formal gardens inspired by those of Spain. The old Southwest trade routes bring us to El Rancho de las Golondrinas and the Garden at El Zaguán in Santa Fe, one with hacienda gardens, the other a Victorian-era city garden, both with awe-inspiring vistas of the Sangre de Cristo Mountains.

Ironwood Terrace Plaza at the Arizona-Sonora Desert Museum

Phoenix: Desert Botanical Garden

LOCATION: WITHIN PAPAGO PARK IN SOUTHEAST PHOENIX

Nestled among the buttes of Papago Park, the Desert Botanical Garden offers a glimpse of desert life with the world's largest and most diverse collection of succulent plants displayed outdoors. More than 20,000 plants of 4,000 different taxa are represented, including 250 rare, threatened, and endangered species from the Southwest and Northern Mexico. The garden's mission is to conserve, study, and educate about arid-land plants of the world, especially succulents and native flora of the Southwest. The garden presents some beautifully designed garden areas, though the main attraction is the plants themselves and how they flourish under harsh growing conditions. A morning spent observing their often-strange shapes and impressively spiny defense systems makes us all the more appreciative of their colorful fruits and delicate, fragrant blossoms.

The garden's site was originally a settlement of the Papago people. In 1914, it became part of the 2,000-acre Papago-Saguaro National Monument. The state took over stewardship when the monument closed in 1930, and the city of Phoenix soon bought the parcel to dedicate as Papago Park. The botanical garden began in 1939 with the aid of two benefactors from the Arizona Cactus and Flora Society. Gustaf Starck, an engineer for the Salt River Valley Water Users Association, donated his collection of 700 cacti and succulents, and Gertrude Divine Webster, who had her own impressive plant collection at her winter estate, contributed $10,000 to develop the infant garden. Carved out of 306 acres, the garden's motto was "not to destroy but to glorify."

By 1940, the collection had grown to over 5,000 plants. During World War II, however, gasoline rationing and the loss of workers closed the garden, though volunteers used their own gas rations to drive out to the garden and water plants whenever they could. Military units dragged caissons through the garden beds and shelled the area during target practice. Despite the toll of war-time, the infrastructure of the garden survived in the basic bones of the paths, the administration building (now Webster Auditorium), and remnants of the scientific collection. In 1947, a dying Gertrude Webster came to the rescue one final time by bequeathing a trust for the garden.

The 1950s were a boom time for the garden as well as the local community. With each decade since, the garden has increased its educational and research programs; in 1985, it became a founding member of the Center for Plant Conservation, a national consortium of botanical gardens and arboreta devoted to identifying and preserving rare and endangered plant species. The 145-acre garden and desert preserve

GARDEN OPEN: 7am–8pm daily May through September; 8am–8pm October through April. Closed Christmas Day
ADMISSION: $7.50 adults, $6.50 seniors, $1.50 children 6-12, children 5 and under free
FURTHER INFORMATION FROM: 1201 N. Galvin Parkway Phoenix, 85008. 480.941.1225 or 480.481.8134 (weekends and after hours)
NEARBY SIGHTS OF INTEREST: Phoenix Zoo, Municipal Stadium

A century plant's tall blooming stalk

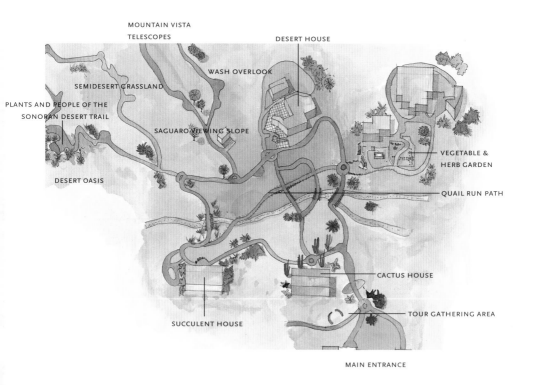

MOUNTAIN VISTA
TELESCOPES

DESERT HOUSE

WASH OVERLOOK

SEMIDESERT GRASSLAND

PLANTS AND PEOPLE OF THE
SONORAN DESERT TRAIL

SAGUARO VIEWING SLOPE

VEGETABLE &
HERB GARDEN

DESERT OASIS

QUAIL RUN PATH

CACTUS HOUSE

SUCCULENT HOUSE

TOUR GATHERING AREA

MAIN ENTRANCE

includes some of the last remnants of natural desert in the Phoenix area. Individual garden areas range from the Rhuart demonstration garden that displays attractive desert plants for home landscapes to ethnobotanical areas such as the Plants and People of the Sonoran Desert Trail. Recent restoration and landscaping efforts have created a handsomely designed network of stone paths, paved trails, benches, water fountains, shaded patios, and ramadas.

The brick-paved Desert Discovery Trail leads one-third of a mile to all the garden's trails and facilities, and features the garden's oldest plantings and exhibits, such as the Cactus House and Succulent House. The beautifully illustrated *A Visitor's Guide to 20 Plants on the Desert Discovery Trail* points out some of the highlights. Beginning near the main entrance, you'll find Arizona Queen of the Night, a slender, stick-like cactus with large, fragrant, trumpet-shaped blossoms that bloom only one night and then die. Contrary to its name, the Parry's century plant (*Agave parryi*) usually lives from seven to 55 years, producing a single flower stalk that rapidly grows up to 35 feet; energy and water spent, it dies. The prickly pear cacti (noted for their fruit, which produce tasty juice that can be enjoyed at the garden's café) bear often whimsical names that describe the shape of their pads, such as cow's tongue and bunny ears. The garden's three tall and hairy boojum trees—the name derives from Lewis Carroll's *Hunting of the Snark,* referring to a mythical being found in far-off regions—are drought-deciduous; they shed their leaves in summer to conserve water. Hummingbirds are attracted to the Baja fairy duster, a shrub with delicate fan-like red blooms that is becoming a popular desert landscaping plant. Fat barrel cacti wear dense wooly caps to protect their tender growing tips from hot sun and freezing temperatures. As you approach the entrance again, peak beneath the shade screens to view the collection of tiny pincushion cacti that in the wild need the shade of large trees or other plants as protection against the sun's rays.

A variety of cacti species that typify the Desert Botanical Garden's collection

Three additional trails provide perspectives on life in the desert. The Plants and People of the Sonoran Desert Trail shows how native peoples used desert plants for food, fiber, and construction. This interactive trail, a third of a mile long, is perfect for families with children who would like to try their hands at pounding mesquite beans into flour or twisting agave fibers to make twine. The quarter-mile Sonoran Desert Nature Trail ascends to an overlook with dramatic vistas of distant mountains and close-up views of the surrounding desert through scopes. The Center for Desert Living trail exhibits a house and gardens that emphasize water and energy conservation.

GARDEN OPEN: Dawn to dusk
daily

FURTHER INFORMATION FROM:

525 E. Main Street
Mesa 85204.
480.964.7164

2 Mesa: Mormon Temple Gardens

LOCATION: ON OLD MAIN STREET IN MESA, ACROSS FROM PIONEER PARK

The temple gardens for the Church of Jesus Christ of Latter-day
Saints in Mesa are lush and meticulously manicured; a
Technicolor antithesis of the wild xeric gardens found in the
desert a few miles away. The effect of acres of thick green lawn,
reflecting pools, fountains, palm trees, and deep flower beds
surrounding the neo-classical temple is almost like a
Hollywood movie set from the 1920s. In arid Arizona, this truly
is an oasis of mythic, even Biblical, proportions. Located in the
center of a 20-acre park, the gardens contain plants from the
ancient world of the Bible, such as deodar cedars, citrus trees,
and date palms. The extensive use of water in the gardens
refers to the city's ancient history as a mesa irrigated by the prehistoric Montezuma Canal, as depicted in an exhibit in the gardens. Settlers in 1878 discovered the remains of a 230-mile
network of canals, remnants of a once-great civilization known
to the Pima Indians as Ho-Ho-Kam, meaning those who are
gone, who lived in the Salt River Valley until about 1400. The
ancient canals compelled the settlers to stay and farm, and were
used as a framework for their own canals. The Mormon community that built the grand temple and gardens in 1927
included descendants of the original settlers. The visitor center

*A long, lush perennial border
on the temple's west side*

leads to a plaza with a reflecting pool rimmed by colorful annual and perennial flowers. At the end of the pool, just below the temple, is a fountain pool. The plaza is flanked by flower beds and lawns punctuated by orange and olive trees, Italian cypress, and red-flowering bottle brush trees. In December, this area is lit with 600,000 Christmas lights, a display that draws thousands of visitors. Here and elsewhere are nine varieties of palms, including Mexican fan palms, queen palms, and Canary Islands date palms. A raised terrace with rose beds and annuals surrounds the terra-cotta-tiled temple, which has classical elements such as columns and a bas relief. On the west side of the temple is a long perennial border, and beyond another reflecting pool is a cactus garden. With cooling water, expanses of lawn, and refreshing colors and fragrances, the temple gardens provide a place for contemplation and appreciation of the gifts of nature.

3 Superior: Boyce Thompson Arboretum

LOCATION: 60 MILES EAST OF PHOENIX, ON HIGHWAY 60, 3 MILES WEST OF SUPERIOR

GARDEN OPEN: 8am–5pm daily. Closed Christmas Day
ADMISSION: $5 adults, $2 ages 5-12, under 5 free
FURTHER INFORMATION FROM: 37615 Highway 60 Superior 85273-5100. 602.689.2811 or 602.689.2723

Nestled against the sheer red-rock cliffs of Magma Ridge, the Boyce Thompson Arboretum is a National Historic Site and a botanical treasure within a fascinating natural setting of panoramic vistas. In 1924, Colonel William Boyce Thompson, a railroad and mining magnate, founded Arizona's oldest botanical garden in a craggy stretch of the Sonoran Desert. Thompson had led a Red Cross expedition through Siberia to aid Russians fighting Germany in the Eastern Theater. During his trip across the tundra, he found people starving, but was also inspired by their resourceful use of scarce plants. After returning to his mining operation in Superior, he began the arboretum to gather and study the usefulness of plants from the world's deserts for purposes such as food, medicine, fiber, energy, and environmental protection. One of the nation's early proponents of what is now called xeriscape (pronounced zeriskape, derived from the Greek "xeri" for dry), Thompson also meant for visitors to appreciate the beauty of the desert. Seventy-five years later, his arboretum, managed cooperatively by the Arizona State Parks, the University of Arizona, and the Boyce Thompson Arboretum, continues to select, breed, and display drought-tolerant plants. Nearly 2,300 species of trees, shrubs, grasses, succulent plants, and herbaceous perennials can be seen along two miles of trails within the arboretum's 300 acres. Using original maps and the latest computer map-

The red-rock cliffs of the Sonoran Desert provide a dramatic setting for Boyce Thompson Arboretum.

ping techniques, the arboretum in recent years has catalogued and replaced many of the plants along the historic main loop trail, which threads through mesquite and wildflower thickets, citrus coves, and saguaro groves. The trail begins near the cactus gardens, which feature bizarre 40-foot boojum trees (*Idria columnaris*) resembling hairy, upended carrots. The trail passes Ayer Lake, near Picketpost House, Thompson's Spanish-style mansion, then down and around the far northeast section of Magma Ridge. Heading back west, the trail winds through a lush native riparian area fed by Queen Creek. It skirts canyon walls and is shaded by huge cottonwood, walnut, date, fig, pistachio, olive, and tangerine trees. Pomegranate hedges line the drive to an old stone and mortar farmstead, the Clevenger House, set into canyon walls and surrounded by a garden of roses, herbs, and yellow-blooming cat's-claw vine. Continuing west and north, the trail passes through groves of palms and fragrant, towering eucalyptus. Within the restored greenhouses are various spiny, cushiony, and sword-like plants, including endangered *Pereskia grandiflora*. Elsewhere are newer demonstration gardens such as a legume garden and a residential xeriscape garden, and the Chihuahuan Desert Trail, where giant tree yuccas and Texas rain sage offer an interesting contrast to the Sonoran plants.

GARDEN OPEN: 7am–sunset daily

ADMISSION: Free ($2 donation suggested)

FURTHER INFORMATION FROM:
7366 N. Paseo del Norte
Tucson 85704-4415.
520.575.8468

NEARBY SIGHTS OF INTEREST:
Tucson Museum of Art,
Tucson Children's Museum

4 Tucson: Tohono Chul Park

LOCATION: IN NORTH TUCSON, OFF INA ROAD, JUST WEST OF ORACLE

Early morning in Tohono Chul Park is a quietly exhilarating experience, with birdsong, trickling water, dappled sunlight, and night-cooled stone and adobe. Even when the desert's light and heat are at their most intense, the park is an oasis with breezes and shady places to relax beneath the shade of ironwood, palo verdes, and mesquite trees. In the early 1920s, Tohono Chul (meaning "desert corner" in Tohono O'odham) was grazing land and groves of citrus and date palms. The property changed hands several times over the next four decades, during which the adobe-style main house and west house (now the tea room) were built. In 1966, Richard and Jean Wilson, who ran their Haunted Bookshop on the property, began acquiring land and constructed a half-mile desert loop trail, ramadas, demonstration gardens, a recirculating stream, and a geological recreation of the Santa Catalina Mountains. In 1985, as Tucson development encroached, the Wilsons dedicated Tohono Chul Park as a nonprofit desert preserve (11 more acres were added later). Part estate gardens and part nature preserve, the park recalls the richness of the Sonoran Desert and the beauty of this set-

ting in the foothills of the Santa Catalinas,
before it was surrounded by busy roads
and suburban development. At the circular brick entry plaza is an innovative sundial, or "horizontal heliochronometer,"
within a wildflower garden. Leading to the
Wilson's 1937 adobe home, which now
houses a gift shop, exhibit space, and
administrative offices, is a walled Spanish
Colonial courtyard shaded by pomegranate and Texas olive trees and perfumed by
Mexican honeysuckle. On the east side of
the house, a children's garden is detailed
with delightful elements that both stimulate the imagination and encourage exploration of the natural world—birdhouses,
fountains, a runnel "stream" and bright,
interesting plants such as bougainvillea.
To the north are wildlife viewing areas
and a quarter-mile loop trail with luscious
views of the mountains. The Alice
Holsclaw Performance Garden is planted
with flowering herbs and shrubs such as
evening primroses, butterfly bush, and a
grove of sweet acacias. An ethnobotanical garden with an ocotillo paling
fence displays plants cultivated or used by

TOP: *Cacti*
BOTTOM: *An ocotillo fence
marks the ethnobotanical
garden*

the native Southwest peoples, such as a fig trees, jojoba, and
sacred datura. The gnarled and spiny figures of "jumping
cholla" (*Opuntia fulgida*) animate the cholla forest on the site
of the former citrus grove. Southeast of the house are demonstration gardens, the geology wall, a greenhouse, and the
recirculating stream, planted with iris and Arizona sycamore,
velvet ash, and willow trees. Collections of yucca, prickly
pear, pincushion cactus, and other desert plants line the
paths that lead to the south loop nature trail and back to the
entrance. Knowledgeable volunteers regularly give tours of
the gardens. On an early-morning birding tour, for example,
a small group of us were delighted to see a covey of quail
scurry across a dirt path near the ethnobotanical garden.
Hooper's hawks, lesser goldfinch, grosbeaks, cactus wrens,
verdins, house finches, and mourning doves dart and sing
through the garden. Purple-headed Costa's hummingbirds
make their home here year-round, and Anna's and black-
chinned hummers fly through chattering on their migratory
missions. You might catch a glimpse of one of these swift iri-
descent birds hovering over the hummingbird garden's
sages, penstemons, and red bird-of-paradise. Located next to
the tearoom, this garden is a lovely place to relax before or
after your tou.

GARDEN OPEN:

8:30am–4:30pm daily

ADMISSION: $4 adults, $3 seniors, $1 children 6–11, children under 5 free

FURTHER INFORMATION FROM:

2150 N. Alvernon Way

Tucson 85712.

520.326.9686

NEARBY SIGHTS OF INTEREST:

University Museums, Reid Park Zoo

5   # Tucson: Tucson Botanical Gardens

LOCATION: IN THE HEART OF TUCSON, ON ALVERNON WAY, BETWEEN PIMA STREET AND GRANT ROAD

Tucked within the heart of the city, the Tucson Botanical Gardens make the most of their precious space with a procession of 20 intimate, individual gardens that unfold like a series of discoveries. Part historical estate garden and part botanical adventure, they offer many rich plant and design ideas appropriate to the scale of most residential gardens. The entrance, patio, and historical gardens surrounding the adobe house (now the visitor center) provide a glimpse of how Rutger and Bernice Porter lived from the late 1920s until the mid-1960s. Rutger was a nurseryman, and he and Bernice created an amazingly diverse oasis of formal and informal gardens on what had been acres of creosote bushes and mesquite trees (the reception garden still displays the cattle tank used for irrigation water in the 1930s and 40s). Their gardens included many trees, vines, and perennials, notably ivy, lilacs, and roses. In 1968, well on in years, the couple donated their home and five-and-a-half acres to the botanical garden. Since then, the botanical gardens have built an education center, a tropical greenhouse exhibit, and numerous small gardens, from an herb garden with a classical fountain, to a children's garden, to a sensory garden with plant-filled ramadas devoted to the five senses. Details such as carved concrete benches inlaid with bright Mexican tiles are handsome decorative touches. Part of the mission is to show how to garden in the desert using appropriate plants and water conservation techniques. Plants and their often-fantastical shapes and textures are critical to the garden designs, especially in the xeriscape and cactus and succulent gardens. An octopus agave, large coral aloes, and a Joshua tree, a form of yucca from the Mojave Desert that looks like a character from Dr. Seuss, are sculptural elements in the xeriscape garden. Elsewhere, grapefruit trees provide dense shade for the picnic area, and a stand of tall spineless cactus (*Opuntea ficus indicus*) forms a wall. Other demonstration gardens include one devoted to native American crops and a Tohono O'odham roundhouse, a ceremonial gathering space built with mesquite, creosote, and saguaro ribs. One of the most beautiful and personal gardens here is one honoring Tucson's Mexican-Americans and their neighborhoods. This barrio garden is filled with roses, annual flowers spilling out of olive oil cans and washtubs, hand-lettered signs, and devotional displays. Nearby mixes of native

African succulents, young saguaro, and shrubs in Rodney Engard Cactus and Succulent Garden

lupines, and Mexican gold poppies bloom in the wildflower and butterfly gardens. In the bird garden, the Cape honeysuckle's orange trumpet flowers attract birds without the use of traditional feeders. One of the birds' favorite nesting spots is in the crested saguaro, a rare variant of the giant saguaro with a bird-like crest on its head. Inside the cactus' body, which is insulated by thousands of gallons of water, the birds build nests that are walled off from each other like a desert skyscraper for winged creatures.

6 Tucson: Arizona-Sonora Desert Museum

LOCATION: IN FOOTHILLS WEST OF DOWNTOWN TUCSON; SPEEDWAY BOULE-VARD EXIT ON I-10, WEST ON GATES PASS ROAD, RIGHT (NORTH) ON KINNEY ROAD 2.5 MILES TO MUSEUM

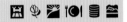

GARDEN OPEN: 7:30am–6pm March through September; 8:30am–5pm October through February
ADMISSION: $8.95 adults; $1.75 children 6-12; children under 6 free
FURTHER INFORMATION FROM: 2021 North Kinney Road Tucson 85743-8919. 520.883.2702
NEARBY SIGHTS OF INTEREST: Saguaro National Park, Old Tucson Studios

A scenic hour's drive west of downtown Tucson through the Tucson Mountains, the Arizona-Sonora Desert Museum is a combination of natural history museum, zoo, and botanical garden. More than 300 species of animals and 1,380 kinds of plants are exhibited at the museum in settings mimicking their natural habitats. A private, nonprofit, educational institution, the museum is dedicated to fostering public appreciation and wise stewardship of the Sonoran Desert region. The garden's mission since its founding in 1950 has been to show the inter-relationships among the region's land, water, plants, wildlife, and people. Located on a ridge between the Sonoran and Mojave deserts, with only 12 inches of rain in an average year, the region is nevertheless rich in flora and fauna. Six different ecosystems are represented in the trails and displays that encompass 21 of the more than 97 acres the museum leases from Pima County. The main trail is one-and-a-half-miles long. From the overlook west of the entrance you can see Boboquieri Peak, sacred to the Tohono O'odham Indians, whose reservation lies in the valley. The trail winds down a slope through various ecosystem displays including mountain woodland, desert grassland, and riparian corridor. The half-mile desert or Arizona uplands loop allows for an intimate view of the desert and sweeping views westward across the gray-green seas of the Avra and Altar valleys. In the cactus garden, and beyond in the desert, are the giant saguaros—many of them up to a century old—that are native only to this region. The

The cactus garden at the Arizona-Sonora Desert Museum

pollination gardens offer some colorful and interesting flower combinations. My favorite is the hummingbird aviary, where seven species of these tiny swift birds swoop freely among visitors. Since the aviary was installed in 1988, nesting hummers have produced more than 106 fledglings. A bee ramada features 1,000 kinds of native bees; a moth garden displays night pollinators such as white desert primroses; and a butterfly garden grows purple desert four-o'clocks, orange lantana, and milkweed. Shade ramadas throughout the garden provide a respite from the intense desert sun, though it's also wise to wear a hat and sunscreen. Picnicking is not allowed, but a coffee bar, café, and restaurant with some outdoor seating offer places to relax and eat. A desert garden nearby shows elegant residential xeriscape designs, and a red garden lights up with fiery hues of scarlet sage and coral bean. Indoor exhibits such as those on reptiles and wildflowers provide a closer look at some of the desert's more elusive plants and animals.

GARDEN OPEN: 9am–5pm Monday–Saturday.
ADMISSION: Free
FURTHER INFORMATION FROM:
Historic Santa Fe Foundation
545 Canyon Road
Santa Fe 87501.
505.983.2567
NEARBY SIGHTS OF INTEREST:
Historic downtown Santa Fe and museums, art galleries along Canyon Road

7 Santa Fe: Garden at El Zaguán (Bandelier Garden)

LOCATION: ON CANYON ROAD, IN DOWNTOWN SANTA FE

The white picket fence along Canyon Road's almost continuous string of art galleries and old adobe buildings is a visual clue to the Garden at El Zaguán's unusual history. Peering over the fence, you'll find a small English cottage garden with old-fashioned perennial flowers, dirt pathways, and turquoise Victorian wrought-iron furniture. In the distance is the dramatic vista of the Sangre de Cristo Mountains. Recreated by the Historic Santa Fe Foundation in the early 1990s, the garden is thought to have begun in the late-nineteenth century when James Johnson, a successful Santa Fe trader, built the adobe hacienda, now the offices of the Historic Santa Fe Foundation and private apartments. A long narrow building, it features a covered, arched corridor connecting wings of the house with the garden—hence the name El Zaguán, Spanish for "breezeway." Legend has it that on his trading trips back to the midwest via Canyon Road—part of the historic Santa Fe Trail—Johnson would bring back seeds for his garden. Adolph Bandelier, an anthropologist whose research on ancient Indian cliff dwellings brought attention to the nearby majestic (and eponymous) Bandelier National Monument, lived here in 1890-91. (Locally, this garden also is called the Bandelier Garden.) During the garden restoration, two rectangular beds divided by crisscross paths were uncovered and replanted to replicate the design of the early garden. Because of Santa Fe's high altitude and cool nights, many perennials usually associated with cooler climates, such as the garden's century-old pink peonies, can grow here. The color theories of English garden designer Gertrude Jekyll were used to create themes. Near the house are the warm pastels of pink roses, lavender, and peonies framed by deeper hues of delphinium, snapdragons, and lupines. The middle beds brim with bellflowers, salvias, lily-of-the-valley, and daisies, while the beds furthest from the house light up with red-hot poker, heliopsis, and yellow calendulas. Old iris and Santa Fe roses such as the burnished Austrian copper rose and sunny Sevilla add historic native touches. Though the peak bloom time is June and July, the garden is lovely year-round, offering spring bulbs, a shady, restful spot in late summer, and sunny warm winter days to enjoy views of the Sangre de Cristos' snow-capped peaks.

8 Santa Fe: El Rancho de las Golondrinas

LOCATION: ABOUT 15 MILES SOUTH OF SANTA FE, ON LOS PIÑOS ROAD IN LA CIENEGA: TAKE I-25 SOUTH, EXIT 276, THEN FOLLOW SIGNS FOR MUSEUM

El Rancho de las Golondrinas, or The Ranch of the Swallows, has a long legacy in the La Cienega Valley. This historic Spanish colonial ranch was a stopping place or *paraje* for travelers on El Camino Reál (the Royal Road to Mexico City), which was North America's longest and most important trade route. A working farm that has raised agricultural crops for more than two centuries, it was a self-sufficient hacienda. It now is a living history museum depicting Spanish colonial life in New Mexico from 1700 to the mid-1800s, featuring numerous restored structures such as a chapel, a defense tower, and a wheelwright shop. The Baca family owned the land for two centuries, until 1932, when it was purchased by the Curtin-Paloheimo family. In 1972, the Curtin-Paloheimo family gave the land to a charitable trust, which opened the living history museum to educate

GARDEN OPEN: 1pm–4pm Wednesday–Sunday, June through September

ADMISSION: $5 adults, $4 seniors, military, and ages 13-18, $2 ages 5-12, under 5 free

TOURS: Guided tours are offered by advance reservation from April through October

FURTHER INFORMATION FROM: 334 Los Piños Road Santa Fe 87505. 505.471.2261 www.golondrinas.org

BELOW: *Libby's Garden at El Rancho de las Golondrinas*

visitors, especially students, about the culture and history of Spanish Colonial New Mexico. The 200-acre ranch includes pastures and several acres of crops that are indigenous to the Southwestern mountains or were introduced by Spanish colonials, such as heirloom varieties of gourds, Chimayo melon, sorghum, San Juan melon squashes, Navajo blue corn, pumpkins, dried beans, and chili peppers. A small vineyard produces grapes for the winery next door. Leonora Curtin was an ethnobotanist who wrote a book about indigenous plants, and a small botanic garden commemorates her love of plants. At the entrance is the memorial Libby's Garden, designed in four sections with a lawn and ornamental plants such as grasses, day lilies, and peonies. A mountain village herb garden is arranged in two semi-circles of native and introduced herbs used for medicinal, culinary, and dye purposes. The ranch is surrounded by hills on the perimeter, with glorious views of several mountain chains named for their colors at sunset, including the Sangre de Cristo (Blood of Christ) and the Sandias (watermelon) Mountains. An afternoon spent in the gardens and walking the trails through the ranch is restorative and will quickly put you in touch with the spirit of this place.

9   Albuquerque: Rio Grande Botanical Garden

LOCATION: IN OLD TOWN ALBUQUERQUE, NEXT TO THE RIO GRANDE RIVER

GARDEN OPEN: 9am–5pm daily; 9am–6pm summer weekends, closed New Year's Day, Thanksgiving, and Christmas Day
ADMISSION: $4.50 adults; $2.50 seniors and children under 12 (admission price includes entry to both botanic garden and aquarium)
FURTHER INFORMATION FROM: 2601 Central Avenue Albuquerque 87104. 505.764.6200
NEARBY SIGHTS OF INTEREST: Old Town, New Mexico Natural History Museum, Albuquerque Fine Arts Museum, Indian Pueblo Cultural Center

The Rio Grande Botanical Garden is part of a developing cultural and educational complex known as the Albuquerque Biological Park. Located in Albuquerque's historic and cultural center of Old Town, next to the Rio Grande River, the botanic garden is part of a 260-acre site that includes a new aquarium, an aquatic park, and an existing zoo renovated to provide richer natural habitats. Some 85 acres have already been developed, including the new aquarium and ten acres of the 72-acre botanic garden. The botanic garden has been open only since 1997, though a group of local citizens including botanists, landscape architects, and gardeners originated the idea in 1981. In 1986, this group succeeded in winning ballot approval from voters for a municipal botanic garden and zoological complex to be funded over ten years by a quarter-cent gross receipts tax. The botanic garden and aquarium have completed the first phase of construction, which began in 1987. The entire site was designed to portray the path a drop of rain takes as it progresses down the Rio Grande from southern Colorado to the Gulf of Mexico. The layout of the site incorporates elevation changes and indigenous geologic materials such as sandstone to create settings for the displays of animals, birds, fish, and plants. The collection of plants and animals interprets three biomes, or ecological communities, through which the river flows. In the botanic garden, a 10,000 square-foot conservatory with two glass pyramid pavilions is the focal point of the design and the collections. One pavilion features plants from the Mediterranean; the other displays plants from North American deserts, including endangered ones like the saguaro cactus, whose dwindling numbers are found only in Arizona and a small part of southwestern New Mexico. This pavilion, a dramatic passive-solar architectural feature, is situated next to the festival green, which separates the formal gardens from the more informal trails leading to the natural gardens. The formal gardens include a Spanish-Moorish court, a round garden with a lion fountain modeled upon Granada's Alhambra, a ceremonial rose garden, and a demonstration garden with seasonal plantings of annual and perennial flowers. A healing garden features a 17-by-9-foot bronze sculpture by local artist Sunny Rivera depicting a *curandera*, or traditional healer, visiting a family. Surrounding the sculpture are santolina, ginger root, lavender, and mullein plants used for healing in the Native American and Spanish Colonial traditions. The informal gardens include trails depicting desert plant life, with cacti, rabbitbrush, sages, and wildflowers.

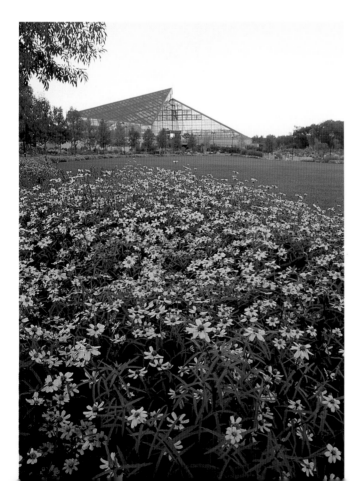

The festival green and conservatory

GARDEN OPEN: Sunrise to
sunset daily

ADMISSION: Free

FURTHER INFORMATION FROM:
Fabian Garcia Science Center
Agricultural Experimentation
Station
PO Box 30003
Las Cruces 88003-0003.
505.646.3638

NEARBY SIGHTS OF INTEREST:
New Mexico State University
campus xeriscapes and
International Mall's unusual
trees

10 Las Cruces: New Mexico State University Landscape Demonstration Garden

LOCATION: ON UNIVERSITY AVENUE NEAR MAIN STREET

At the northern tip of the Chihuahuan Desert, at an elevation of 3,500 feet, the New Mexico State University Landscape Demonstration Garden displays plants that love hot, dry weather and little rain. All 250 species of plants in the one-acre garden at the Fabian Garcia Science Center are from parts of the world with similar high-desert climates. Founded in 1989, its mission is to educate university students and the public about water-wise plants that thrive in this environment—rabbit brush, mesquites, desert honeysuckle, and Texas ranger, a small silver-leafed shrub with lovely purple flowers that bloom from August through the first frost. All the plants are labeled with their Latin names and icons noting whether they are xeric, edible, or attractive to butterflies or birds. In fact, many of the plants do attract unusual and magnificent butterflies, such as common sulfurs, blue skippers, California sisters, and mourning cloaks. The garden is designed with a central axis that leads toward a gazebo and crisscross paths with flower beds in the middle. Perennials are mixed with annuals, which are replanted seasonally, such as snapdragons, pansies, and ornamental kale in winter. Spring blooms with sweet Williams and crabapples. Many of the plants, such as Afghan pine trees and weeping mulberry, were developed by a local professor, and are studied as part of research conducted by the university's Agricultural Experimentation Station. The garden is especially appropriate for children: newer theme gardens include an herb and dye garden, a medicinal garden, and an "earthmath" garden, where children can study classical landscape shapes and dimensions. Across the street on two-and-a-half acres, an agronomic maze is planted each year with tall corn or millet and hidden lessons for children to uncover related to the history of the region.

11 Carlsbad: Living Desert Zoo & Gardens State Park

LOCATION: NORTH EDGE OF CARLSBAD ON HIGHWAY 285

Living Desert Zoo & Gardens is a zoological and botanical state park that specializes in native species of the Chihuahuan Desert. Though it may seem an arid wasteland, with extreme heat and only 10 inches of rain per year, the Chihuahuan Desert supports hundreds of species of plants, trees, and wildlife. Located about 30 miles from the Texas border, the park encompasses approximately 1,100 acres within the northern reaches of the desert, with 45 acres maintained for zoo and garden exhibits. Near the entrance to the park, the visitor center includes interpretive displays, administrative offices, and other facilities. A one-and-one-third-mile self-guided walking tour begins just outside the visitor center and introduces visitors to various habitats found in the region. The Sand Hills depict an area east of Carlsbad where sand deposits support plants with extensive root systems, such as yucca, mesquite, and sand sage. The desert uplands are outfitted with prickly pear cactus and furniture cholla, so named because their thick, hollow, dead stalks are used for furniture and lamps. The desert arroyo, a ditch carved by water in the desert, supports thick vegetation, including agaves and sotols. And the piñon-juniper zone, representative of elevations of 4,500-6,000 feet, looks like mountain islands in a desert sea, where sagebrush, bear grass, piñon pines, and junipers thrive. This trail also shows off the native desert marigolds, Mexican gold poppies, and blanket flowers. The ocotillo overlook is spectacular in April and May, when clusters of the ocotillo's fiery tubular flowers attract scores of hummingbirds. On a clear day, the view from the overlook extends many miles across the lower Pecos Valley. Along the same trail, you can view the reptile exhibit, the aviary's raven, wild turkey, and mourning doves, mammals of the desert such as elk, pronghorn, bison, and Mexican wolf, and an exhibit featuring nocturnal reptiles and amphibians. A waterfowl pond is home to mallards, teals, and blue herons during the winter months. The park's biggest crowds are during its hottest period in summer, though native cacti and succulents bloom from early spring through late fall. The park's greenhouse, a popular attraction, offers a wide variety of native and exotic plants, including collections of euphorbias, ice plants, and succulents from far-off regions like Madagascar. Two adjoining, smaller greenhouses are used to propagate native plants for the park and for sale in the gift shop, located at the visitor center. Near the greenhouse, a new xeriscape garden brims with water-wise flowers and shrubs—black and feather dahlias, Tahoka daisies, and prostrate rosemary.

GARDEN OPEN: 8am–8pm daily Memorial Day through Labor Day; 9am–5pm Labor Day through Memorial Day; closed Christmas Day

ADMISSION: $4 adult, $2 children 7-12, children 6 and under free

FURTHER INFORMATION FROM: P.O. Box 100 1504 Miehls Drive Carlsbad 88221-0100. 505.887.5516 www.carlsbadnm.com

NEARBY SIGHTS OF INTEREST: Carlsbad Caverns National Park

FORT BRAGG
1

5,6
SACRAMENTO
RENO
40

SANTA ROSA 2
3
SAUSALITO
BERKELEY 9–13
OAKLAND 14 15
SAN FRANCISCO
7,8
17,18 16
9 PALO ALTO
20

NEVADA

SANTA CRUZ
21

CALIFORNIA

22

LAS VEGAS

HENDERSON
41

SANTA BARBARA
23,24
25
28 27
29
LOS ANGELES
31 30 CLAREMONT
26
LONG BEACH
32 33
PALM SPRINGS
34,35

LAGUNA BEACH
36 37
38
SAN DIEGO
39

1 Fort Bragg: Mendocino Coast
Botanical Gardens
2 Santa Rosa: Luther Burbank
Home and Gardens
3 Sausalito: Green Gulch Farm
4 Ross: Marin Art and Garden
Center
5 Davis: Davis Arboretum of the
University of California
6 Sacramento: C.M. Goethe
Arboretum
7 San Francisco: Golden Gate Park
8 San Francisco: Strybing
Arboretum and Botanical
Gardens
9 Berkeley: University of California
Botanical Garden
10 Berkeley: Berkeley Rose Garden

11 Berkeley: Blake Garden
12 Berkeley: Regional Parks Botanic
Garden
13 El Cerrito: The Harland Hand
Garden
14 Oakland: Morcom Amphitheater
of Roses
15 Walnut Creek: The Ruth Bancroft
Garden
16 Menlo Park: Sunset Gardens
17 Woodside: Filoli
18 Palo Alto: The Elizabeth F.
Gamble Garden Center
19 Saratoga: Hakone Gardens
20 Saratoga: Villa Montalvo
21 Santa Cruz: University of
California at Santa Cruz
Arboretum

22 San Simeon: Hearst San Simeon
State Historical Monument
23 Santa Barbara: Santa Barbara
Botanic Garden
24 Santa Barbara: Ganna Walska
Lotusland
25 Beverly Hills: Robinson Gardens
26 Los Angeles: Mildred E. Mathias
Botanical Garden
27 La Cañada Flintridge: Descanso
Gardens
28 San Marino: Huntington
Botanical Gardens
29 Arcadia: The Arboretum of Los
Angeles County
30 Claremont: Rancho Santa Ana
Botanic Garden
31 Palos Verdes: South Coast

Botanic Garden
32 Long Beach: Rancho Los
Alamitos
33 Fullerton: Fullerton Arboretum
34 Palm Springs: Moorten
Botanical Garden
35 Palm Desert: The Living Desert
36 Corona Del Mar: Sherman
Library and Gardens
37 Laguna Beach: Hortense Miller
Garden
38 Encinitas: Quail Botanical
Gardens
39 San Diego: Balboa Park
40 Reno: Wilbur D. May Arboretum
& Botanical Garden
41 Henderson: Ethel M. Chocolate
Factory Botanical Garden

FAR WEST

California, Nevada

California is a gardener's paradise, with a moderate climate and winters warm enough to encourage year-round blooms in all but the highest elevations. The public gardens in the Golden State are among the finest examples from three centuries of landscape design. They celebrate several garden traditions: part native—honoring indigenous plants used by local Indians; part European—with classical formal gardens, and Mediterranean architecture and plants and part pioneer spirit—inspired by garden styles brought from the East or Midwest. As a gateway to the Pacific, California also welcomed plants from China and Japan from the nineteenth century on. Since the mid-twentieth century, California gardens have developed a style all their own, often with an eclectic mix of natives plants and those introduced from around the world, as well as designs that express the modern, relaxed, California style of linking interiors with outdoor garden rooms. Gardens such as Rancho Los Alamitos in Long Beach reference centuries of cultural history, from ancient Indian settlements, to traditional European-style gardens, to the gracious yet comfortable and relaxed spaces of a modern California ranch.

The California gardens range from collections of heathers and rhododendrons on bluffs along the northern coast to desert gardens in the inland foothills of Southern California. From the grand estates of Filoli in Woodside and The Huntington in San Marino, to gardens on an acre or two that express one gardener's personal vision, but they all share the ability to display a sumptuous palette of plants from their own region and more exotic locales. For many of these gardens, the mild coastal climate provides the perfect conditions for plants that originated in the Mediterranean regions and other sun-drenched parts of the world. In the drier gardens inland and further south, the often dramatic and bizarre forms of dry-land plants from Mexico, South Africa, South America, Australia, and New Zealand bloom along with natives such as wild lilacs.

Nevada's gardens are even higher and drier, displaying trees, cacti, and succulents that thrive in high-desert conditions. Both Nevada gardens honor their twentieth-century benefactors. Located in a transitional zone between the Sierra Nevada Mountains and the Great Basin Desert, the Wilbur D. May Botanical Garden in Reno receives only seven inches of precipitation a year and has a growing season of less than 100 days. At an elevation of 4,600 feet, the garden's daily temperature can vary 50 degrees or more. At the Ethel M. Chocolate Factory Botanical Garden in Henderson, half the plants are cacti and succulents native to the Southwest, and the rest are desert trees and shrubs from the Southwest, Australia, and South America. Nevada's gardens are well-focused on plants chosen for their aesthetic qualities and their ability to adapt to southern Nevada's hot, dry climate.

Fort Bragg: Mendocino Coast Botanical Gardens

LOCATION: ON THE OCEAN SIDE OF HIGHWAY 1, 2 MILES SOUTH OF FORT BRAGG

The Mendocino Coast Botanical Gardens enjoy a rarefied and beautiful location: fronting the Pacific Ocean on California's rugged northern coast. The borrowed scenery of rocky shore-line, crashing waves, and changing skies is a dramatic setting for these 47 acres of gardens. Sheltered by a native coastal pine forest, they include both manicured formal gardens and natural areas such as a fern-filled canyon and a rocky inter-tidal habitat. The gardens' maritime climate—featuring mild rainy winters and cool foggy summers—provides ideal grow-ing conditions for a dozen extensive collections of plants such as camellias, dahlias, fuchsias, heather, and rhododen-drons. The gardens were begun as a labor of love. In 1961, Ernest Schoefer, a retired nurseryman, and his wife Betty bought the property and began the arduous task of clearing, planting, and trail building. The Schoefers supported their endeavors with a retail nursery, gift shop, and $1 admission. By 1992, the Mendocino Coast Recreation and Park District was able to purchase the entire property for use as a public botanical garden with grants from the California State Coastal Conservancy. The gardens are operated as a public trust, nonprofit member organization. More than three miles of trails wind through the individual gardens, beginning with perennials, ivies, heritage roses, heathers, and succulents. Between the main north and south trails is a shaded wood-land, a fuchsia garden, a marsh, and several collections of rhododendrons, including tender species rhododenrons and others that tower to 20 feet. The trails skirt Digger Creek's fern canyon and a dahlia garden and eventually arrive at a meadow. The coastal bluff trail loops around to the cliff house for views of the ocean, seals playing in the water, and migrating gray whales. The gardens are home to a wildlife community that includes river otters, foxes, and more than 100 species of birds. Its mild climate allows blooms year-round—camellias, magnolias, Pacific Coast iris, and daf-fodils brighten the gardens as early as February, and Japanese maples and heathers warm them through the winter.

GARDEN OPEN: 9am–5pm daily March through October, 9am–4pm November through February, closed Saturday after Labor Day and Thanksgiving and Christmas Day

ADMISSION: $6 adult, $5 senior, $3 ages 13–17, $1 ages 6–12, children under 5 free

FURTHER INFORMATION FROM: 18220 N. Highway 1 Fort Bragg 95437. 707.964.4352 www.gardensbythesea.org

The dramatic vista of the Pacific from Mendocino Coast Botanical Gardens

GARDEN OPEN: Dawn to dusk
daily

ADMISSION: Free

TOURS OF HOUSE: 10am–
3:30 pm every half-hour,
Tuesday–Sunday, April 1
through October 31; $3
adults, children 12 and under
free

FURTHER INFORMATION FROM:
P.O. Box 1678
Santa Rosa 95402.
707.524.5445
www.lutherburbank.org

NEARBY SITES OF INTEREST:
Sonoma County Museum

2 Santa Rosa: Luther Burbank Home and Gardens

LOCATION: DOWNTOWN SANTA ROSA, AT THE CORNER OF SANTA ROSA AVENUE
AND SONOMA AVENUE

Shasta daisies are the best-known of more than 800 varieties of
plants that Luther Burbank (1849–1926) introduced. Born in
Lancaster, Massachusetts, Burbank was living there as a young
man when he introduced his first important horticultural discovery: the Burbank potato, a firm, dependable, blight-resistant spud
whose descendents are Idaho bakers. Upon moving to the West
coast, he opened a nursery in Santa Rosa in 1877, dedicating the
next 50 years to hybridizing fruits, vegetables, and flowers. Here
at his home and garden and on a farm in nearby Sebastopol, the
famed horticulturist—by now known as the "Plant Wizard"—
conducted experiments that improved plant performance and
helped revolutionize food production and preservation worldwide. In the decades following his death in 1926, his widow,
Elizabeth, sold off all but one-and-a-half of the original four acres,
which became a public garden in 1960. Upon her death in 1977,
Elizabeth Burbank bequeathed the property to the city of Santa
Rosa. A National Historic Landmark, it includes Burbank's clapboard Greek revival house and his greenhouse, both open for
docent-led tours, for a small admission fee. The gardens display
many of his introductions. The rose garden near the main
entrance, for example, features *Rosa multiflora* "thornless" roses
around a fountain. A small orchard just east of the carriage house
contains some of the 200 varieties of Burbank's fruit and nut
trees, such as the Santa Rosa plum, the paradox walnut, and the
"plumcot," a cross between a plum and an apricot. Next to them
are lilies, dahlias, zinnias, gladiolus, and various vegetables and
herbs displayed in raised demonstration beds with his famed
Shasta daisies, which took 17 years to pro-
duce. Burbank experimented over 20 years
with many cacti, creating spineless ones that
could provide forage for cattle in the desert.
In the drought-tolerant garden are poppies
and other native varieties related to those
Burbank bred to enhance flower size, fragrance, or color. An old-fashioned border
garden along the front lawn includes lilacs,
spirea, saucer magnolias, among other
annuals and perennials popular in the late
1800s. Here and elsewhere on the grounds
are examples of his showy canna hybrids
such as the King Humbert, as well as amar-
crinum, a hybrid of his giant amaryllis and
the crinium lily.

*The carriage house at the
Luther Burbank Home and
Gardens*

3 Sausalito: Green Gulch Farm

LOCATION: ON SHORELINE HIGHWAY 1, 4.5 MILES FROM HIGHWAY 101, STIN-
SON BEACH EXIT

GARDEN OPEN: 9am–4pm
daily
ADMISSION: Free
FURTHER INFORMATION FROM:
1601 Shoreline Highway
Sausalito 94965.
415.383.3134

Enfolded in a secluded valley that opens onto Muir Beach and the Pacific Ocean, Green Gulch Farm is worlds away from the bustle of San Francisco just 17 miles to the south. Redwoods, Monterey pines, live oaks, and eucalyptus trees line the steep single-lane road that leads from Highway 1 to the farm, a Buddhist practice and retreat center in the Japanese Soto Zen tradition. The farm was founded in 1972 after George Wheelwright sold part of his cattle ranch to the San Francisco Zen Center with the provision that the center always promote sensitive agricultural practices and remain open to the public. The original gardens were started in the early 1970s by Alan Chadwick, the renowned advocate of organic, biointensive farming, who lived here until 1972 and returned just before his death in 1980 (a simple stupa on the farm marks his grave). The current garden is inspired by and dedicated to Chadwick, and through experimentation and hard work it has become beautiful and productive. Of the center's 115 acres, one-and-a-half are ornamental gardens of herbs, flowers, and fruit trees, arranged in a series of "rooms" in the formal English style. In the bowl of the valley is the core of the gardens: an herbal circle of shrubs, roses, and perennials, enclosed by a yew hedge with rose arbors and paths out to the larger garden. At the center of the circle is a Japanese snowbell (*Styrax japonica*) encircled by herbs and lichen-covered rocks. A meditation garden features three types of trees—Mugo pine, bamboo, and cherry, known as the Three Friends (*sho–chiku–bai* in Japanese). They symbolize Zen attributes of strength, flexibility, and transient beauty. The farm includes eight acres of organic vegetable beds that supply the Zen center, local farmers markets, and Greens restaurant in San Francisco. A nursery within the garden sells organic shrubs and perennials. An inholding of the Golden Gate National Recreation Area, the landscape is replete with native plants and wildlife. The Zen center encourages an atmosphere of peacefulness and quiet; birdcalls, wind, and other songs of nature can be heard throughout the grounds. Muir Beach is a 15-minute walk through the gardens and fields, and miles of easy hiking trails connect Green Gulch to Muir Woods, Mt. Tamalpais, the Golden Gate Bridge, and Stinson Beach.

The garden spans the valley floor leading to the Pacific.

GARDEN OPEN: Dawn to dusk
daily
ADMISSION: Free
FURTHER INFORMATION FROM:
P.O. Box 437
30 Sir Francis Drake
Boulevard
Ross 94957–0437.
415.454.5597
www.marinartandgarden.org

The Moya Library

4 Ross: Marin Art and Garden Center

LOCATION: 30 SIR FRANCIS DRAKE BOULEVARD, AT THE INTERSECTION OF LAU-
REL GROVE AVENUE

Located in an historic area close to downtown Ross, the Marin
Art and Garden Center spans ten acres of manicured grounds
with large specimen trees, shrubs, and flowers. The site has a
long and interesting history of its own: in 1840, it was given to
Captain Juan B.R. Cooper by the Mexican Governor of
California for use as a ranch. Seventeen years and two owners
later, it was purchased by James Ross of Inverness, Scotland,
who with his wife Annie established a trading post. Beginning
in 1863, their daughter Annie and her husband George A.
Worn lived on the ranch, built a home and an octagonal pump
house, and planted extensive gardens. When a subsequent
owner wished to sell the property to a subdivision developer in
1943, Caroline Livermore organized eight community groups
to buy the property. Today, the Marin Art and Garden Center
is operated on a nonprofit basis and is home to numerous
organizations, including local garden clubs, a theater group,
and an art society. Paths lead through the grounds to places
both public and private, such as secluded dells with benches

sheltered by birch, laurel, holly, and rhododendron. The garden retains many of the original trees, such as a giant sequoia located in Pixie Park, a playground near an amphitheater and barn. The region's mild, Mediterranean climate encourages a wide variety of trees, from English oak to pineapple guava, and it allows for year-round color and texture, with spring-flowering plums and magnolias, warm fall tones of maples and oaks, and the winter beauty of spruces, cedars, and holly. A fountain near the Octagon House (now home to the Ross Historical Society) displays an apple tree and wisteria, and elsewhere are other old-fashioned favorites such as weigela, lilacs, and crape myrtle. The memory garden, a tribute to deceased Marin residents, was created by the Marin Garden Club as a quiet place for meditation, featuring an astrological sundial, an oriental lantern, and statues.

5 Davis: Davis Arboretum of the University of California

LOCATION: AT THE SOUTHERN EDGE OF THE CAMPUS, OFF ROUTE 80, UC DAVIS EXIT

GARDEN OPEN: Dawn to dusk daily

ADMISSION: Free

FURTHER INFORMATION FROM:
Davis Arboretum
University of California
Davis 95616.
530.752.4880
www.arboretum.ucdavis.edu

The Davis Arboretum of the University of California stretches along 100 acres of the ancient Putah Creek in California's Central Valley. Located 70 miles east of San Francisco, Davis has a climate of extremes, ranging in temperature from 14 degrees Fahrenheit to 118, with an average annual rainfall of only 19 inches. Its hot dry summers and cool wet winters are perfect for plants native to or adapted for Mediterranean climates, a particular focus of this garden. In addition to teaching horticulture and landscape architecture students, part of its mission is to test new plants that do well in the Central Valley and to demonstrate the landscaping use of drought-tolerant, disease-resistant, and low-maintenance plants. The arboretum was founded in 1936 to strengthen the school's biological sciences departments. Faculty members planted many native trees and shrubs in the late 1930s, including a redwood grove that is the largest cultivated collection in the state's interior. In the 1950s, the arboretum was divided into geographic and taxonomic collections, and began building notable collections of oaks, acacias, and eucalyptus. Today paths wind through the garden past scenic lagoons and picnic sites and across footbridges, to take in some 21,000 plants of more than 4,000 taxa. A series of gardens represent horticultural themes and historic periods, as well as plant groups and geographic areas. The Mary Wattis Brown Garden of California natives showcases an extensive collection of wild lilacs (*Ceanothus*), as well as rare

and endangered plants. The Ruth Risdon Storer Garden features roses, flowering perennials, and small shrubs well suited for Central Valley gardens. In the Carolee Shields White Flower Garden, based on the medieval moon-viewing gardens of India and Japan, curving paths frame a vine-covered gazebo with luminous night-blooming flowers. An early California garden displays cultivated natives and plants from Spain and Mexico found on a typical ranch in the mid-1800s, when California was part of Mexico. A horticultural test garden of Australian plants offers shrubs and perennials not yet widely available. Surrounding a lagoon are medicinal and culinary herbs and other plants from Mediterranean climes, including southern Europe, South Africa, Chile, and western Australia.

GARDEN OPEN: Dawn to dusk daily

ADMISSION: Free

FURTHER INFORMATION FROM:
Department of Biological Sciences
California State University
6000 J Street
Sacramento 95819–6077.
916.278.6494

6 Sacramento: C.M. Goethe Arboretum

LOCATION: ON NORTH END OF THE CALIFORNIA STATE UNIVERSITY CAMPUS, NEXT TO THE MAIN ENTRANCE

Located next to the main entrance of the university campus, the three acres of grounds at the C.M. Goethe Arboretum are a fitting gateway and a living museum of the region's trees, shrubs, and perennial plants. Established in 1965 with money donated by C.M. Goethe, a local philanthropist, the arboretum focuses on California natives and other plants from around the world that thrive in Sacramento's dry, hot, 100+ degree summers. About a third of the arboretum is devoted to California natives, including a dozen species of manzanitas. The arboretum is used extensively for teaching botany students, and its mission is to acquaint them with natives and other xeric plants from South Africa, South America, and Australia. Established in an old pear orchard on rich alluvial soil, the arboretum displays 600 species of trees and shrubs, including many cedars, pines, and other conifers. In springtime, it is flush with magnolia blossoms and the blooms of fruit and nut trees such as pistachio, almond, plum, and Japanese flowering cherry. Currants and other fruit-bearing shrubs attract birds, and mock orange, jasmine, and honeysuckle send lovely fragrances wafting through the grounds. In the fall and winter, arborvitae, viburnums, hollies, and witch hazels provide color and texture. Laid out on level land with asphalt paths, the garden is an easy stroll and is accessible to visitors in wheelchairs.

ABOVE: *A serene Central Valley view at the Davis Arboretum*

7 San Francisco: Golden Gate Park

LOCATION: IN NORTHWEST SAN FRANCISCO

In 1868, the City of San Francisco purchased 1,000 acres of windswept dunes on the western side of the city for $800,000. At the time, many citizens believed it a waste of money: lacking water, the land was an unlikely place for a large city park. Then, in 1887, John McLaren, a Scottish landscaper, was appointed superintendent of parks for the city. Over the next 55 years, until his death at age 96 in 1943, McLaren, a well-regarded horticulturist and forester with a reputation for persistence, transformed Golden Gate into one of the most beautiful and unusual parks in the country. Often working from dawn to dusk seven days a week, he dedicated his life to the park, growing more than 2 million trees and shrubs, and creating meadows, lakes, and groves. The park today provides sports and recreation facilities such as boating, tennis, golf, and horseback riding, as well as hundreds of acres of gardens. Free maps are available at park headquarters in the McLaren Lodge at 501 Stanyan Street, near the park entrance. Just west of the lodge are several gardens devoted to fuchsias, camellias, and dahlias. In Conservatory Valley, the Victorian-style glass Conservatory of Flowers, erected in 1878, is one of the park's most visited and photographed places (even though it has been closed since 1995 for rebuilding). Inspired by Kew Gardens in London, it is a magnificent structure surrounded by formal flower beds. The John McLaren Rhododendron Dell features a collection begun by the park superintendent, who knew many of the world's great rhododendron collectors and hybridizers. Planted after his death, the 20-acre garden now contains more than 300 hybrids and 70 species. South of the dell are an AIDS memorial grove, a calm setting for meditation amidst red-

GARDENS OPEN: Dawn to dusk daily (Japanese Tea Garden: 8:30am–6pm daily)

ADMISSION: Free (Japanese Tea Garden: $3.50 adults, $1.25 seniors and ages 6-12)

FURTHER INFORMATION FROM:
McLaren Lodge
Golden Gate Park
501 Stanyan Street
San Francisco 94117-1898.
415.831.2700

NEARBY SITES OF INTEREST:
California Academy of Sciences, Asian Art Museum, M.H. de Young Museum, all within park

The romantic Shakespeare Garden's apple trees

woods, ferns, and dogwoods, and the Shakespeare Garden, a charming garden room with an allée of apple trees and a brick walkway flanked by beds of primrose and lavender. Bronze plaques on a wall are engraved with the bard's verses celebrating various plants. The Strybing Arboretum offers world-class collections of trees, shrubs, and plants. Just north of it is the Japanese Tea Garden, constructed as a Japanese village for the Midwinter International Exposition of 1894. A wealthy Japanese landscape gardener, Makoto Hagiwara, designed and constructed the rural-style landscape and teahouse for the village, later expanding the gardens from one to five acres and running the teahouse as a concession until he died in 1925. His family continued to manage the teahouse and garden until 1942, when the War Department relocated them and the Park Department assumed management. Northwest of the tea garden is the rose garden, dedicated in 1961 with more than 600 rose bushes including heirloom varieties as well as exotic and rare blooms. Flowering beneath the shadow of an immense Dutch windmill at the far western portion of the park near the Pacific Ocean is the Queen Wilhelmina tulip garden, with delightful masses of bright pink, red, yellow, white, and purple flowers in spring.

The rose garden at Golden Gate Park

8 San Francisco: Strybing Arboretum and Botanical Gardens

LOCATION: WITHIN GOLDEN GATE PARK, AT NINTH AVENUE AND LINCOLN WAY

GARDEN OPEN: 8am–4:30pm Monday–Friday, 10am–5pm Saturday, Sunday, and holidays

ADMISSION: Free (donations encouraged)

Tours: Weekdays at 1:30 and weekends at 10:30 & 1:30, free

FURTHER INFORMATION FROM: Strybing Arboretum Society Ninth Avenue at Lincoln Way San Francisco 94122.

415.661.1316

www.strybing.org

Within San Francisco's Golden Gate Park, a 1,000-acre green belt that extends from the Haight-Ashbury district to the Pacific Ocean, is a botanical treasure: the Strybing Arboretum and Botanical Gardens. The Bay Area's mild temperatures, wet winters, and rainless but foggy summers allow for a diverse range of microclimates in the 55-acre gardens. More than 7,000 varieties of plants hail from the New World cloud forests of Central and South America to the Mediterranean climates of Africa, Asia, Australia, New Zealand, and Europe. Plans for an arboretum were part of the original survey for the park in the 1870s, but they became a reality when Helene Strybing, widow of a wealthy San Francisco merchant, left the city of San Francisco a bequest for an arboretum and botanical garden. Work began in the 1930s under the Works Progress Administration, with some of the earliest plants relocated from within the park, including a few specimens that had come from the New Zealand pavilion at the 1915 Panama-Pacific Exposition. The gardens officially opened in 1940. In 1957, a master plan by Robert Tetlow shaped the central lawn and mapped out the geographical areas. Since then the gardens have continued to expand with an emphasis on geographic collections and the conservation of endangered plant species, with the help of the nonprofit Strybing Arboretum Society. The new main entry garden by designers Roger Raiche and Dave McCrory spans two beds nearly 60 feet long and 10 feet wide that flank the walkway with plants whose foliage offers striking year-round color and textures, such as bamboos, tree ferns, orchids, grasses, dracaenas, and mosaics of ground covers. The oval-shaped main lawn and the fountain beyond it are connected by paths to some 17 themed gardens—including a children's garden, a Biblical garden, a fragrance garden, a Japanese-inspired moon viewing and waterfall garden—as well as plant collections from around the world. A color-coded map locates and describes all 24 gardens and their climates and is available for $1 at the information desk. The gardens' magnolias and rhododendrons draw thousands of visitors in the spring. Among the most extensive and unusual collections are those devoted to proteas, heathers, South African bulbs, Chilean plants, including the magnificent mayten tree, lilies, and belleflowers, and the colorful flax, hebes, and red-flowering Christmas trees of New Zealand. My favorite gardens include one devoted to native California plants that features a circular limestone plaza with benches surrounded by rocks, wildflowers, and shrubs, with early summer blooms of sky-blue penstemons, orange poppies, mariposa lilies, and yuccas. Another is devoted to succulents such as gigantic orange-flowering aloes, striped agaves, barrel cactus, and turquoise-flowering puyas that spill over terraced limestone walls and attract hummingbirds, butterflies, and woodpeckers. A garden of Mexican perennials blooms into fall with hot-colored dahlias, primroses, cupheas, and marigolds.

9 Berkeley: University of California Botanical Garden

LOCATION: IN STRAWBERRY CANYON ABOVE THE BERKELEY CAMPUS

GARDEN OPEN: 9am–4:45pm daily, except Christmas Day; 9am–7pm Memorial Day – Labor Day

ADMISSION: Free

TOURS: Free docent-led tours at 1:30pm Thursday, Saturday, and Sunday; group tours by advance arrangement, call 510.642.3352

FURTHER INFORMATION FROM: 200 Centennial Drive Berkeley 94720–5045. 510.643.2755 www.mip.berkeley.edu/garden/

Overlooking San Francisco Bay, and embraced by Strawberry Canyon above the UC Berkeley campus, the University of California Botanical Garden displays one of the world's richest collections of living plants, virtually all of which were collected in the wild or can be traced to wild origins. Strawberry Canyon's mild climate and diverse microhabitats allow plants from around the world to flourish. The garden's 34 acres contain over 10,000 kinds of plants from around the world, arranged geographically and in naturalistic groups that reflect their plant communities and growing conditions. There is also a redwood grove and gardens devoted to herbs, old roses, Chinese medicinal plants, and palms and cycads. Founded in 1890 on the university's central campus, the botanical garden rapidly outgrew its site and in the 1920s was moved to its present location, which had been a dairy farm. The collections grew dramatically as faculty and staff brought back plants from expeditions to the world's farthest reaches. The garden now emphasizes display and education, with numerous programs for school groups and the public. A tour of the garden could begin with the New World Desert collection, one of the oldest, where cacti and other succulents range from tiny Andean cushion plants clinging to rocks

Succulent garden at the Strybing Arboretum

to 35-foot columnar cacti from Argentina. Next to it on a sunny slope are plants from Africa—lilies, iceplants, and aloes that burst forth in spring in nearly neon hues of vermilion, hot pink, purple, orange, and gold. Continuing east up the hill, you'll enter the Asian area through a Japanese-style mountain gate. Overhead are the foot-long clusters of fragrant lavender flowers from an empress tree (*Paulownia glabrata*). A handsome collection of rhododendrons—over 376 species, from tiny pink Nepalese alpines to pale-yellow blooming *lutescens* from China—creates dense layers of foliage along the paths and around a stone-rimmed pool. The South American area features Peruvian lilies, a grove of monkey puzzle trees, and an outstanding collection of fuchsias. Beyond it are the Mediterranean area's rock garden of aromatic herbs and the rose garden's formal beds edged with lavender. From the pergola, you can see the Golden Gate Bridge and (on a clear day) beyond to the Farallon Islands. Under the filtered shade in the Australasian area, you'll find tree ferns and orange-flowering dendrobium orchids. Nearby is a lawn rimmed with Japanese cedars and magnolias featuring herb gardens with more than 200 Chinese medicinal and European herbs. Hummingbirds flock to the fiery tubular flowers of penstemons, salvias, and cestrum in the Mesoamerican area, and in the North American area are classic garden combinations such as moss pink phlox blooming beneath dogwood and tulip trees. About a third of the botanic garden's collection is devoted to California plants, 176 of which are on the state's endangered list. They are displayed here creatively: a serpentine swath of tiny purple alliums and mustard colored wallflowers; a vernal pool with poppies; a pygmy forest of cypress and manzanita. While the garden and its views will most likely keep you outside, you'll find interesting collections in three greenhouses devoted to the desert, ferns and carnivorous plants, and the tropics.

A fanciful bridge at UC Berkeley's Botanical Garden.

53

GARDEN OPEN: Dawn to dusk
daily

ADMISSION: Free

FURTHER INFORMATION FROM:
City of Berkeley Department
of Parks
201 University Avenue
Berkeley 94710.
510.644.6943

10 Berkeley: Berkeley Rose Garden

LOCATION: AT EUCLID AVENUE AND BAYVIEW PLACE, OPPOSITE CODORNICES PARK

Sculpted into a hillside overlooking San Francisco Bay, the historic Berkeley Municipal Rose Garden graces a series of stone terraces hewn from hundreds of tons of native stone quarried in the Berkeley Hills. A joint creation of the City of Berkeley and the Works Progress Administration, the terraced amphitheater and 220-foot-long redwood pergola were suggested by architect Bernard Maybeck; the final design and execution were the work of landscape architect Vernon M. Dean and rose specialist C.V. Covell. Designed in the rustic style, the three-and-a-half-acre garden was built between 1933 and 1937. The East Bay Counties Rose Society selected 2,500 rose bushes and planted them, one color per terrace, in a ribbon-like design that began with red roses at the top and descended through bronze, pink, yellow, to white roses at the bottom. Today, some 3,000 rose bushes of about 250 varieties are mixed in hue. The garden is maintained by the city, with volunteer help and funds from the nonprofit Friends of the Berkeley Rose Garden. A new entry garden was designed by architect Helene Vilett and built with community donations and funds from the city. Paved (but somewhat steep) paths lead through the rose beds. Deep coral Impatiens F tree roses and pure white *Rosa rugosa alba* are memorable blooms on the upper terraces. Around the perimeter of the garden are oaks and cedars, with a bed of poppies and other wildflowers near the south border next to municipal tennis courts. About a third of the way down the terraces, the long curved pergola is covered with such luscious climbing roses as the peach-colored Royal Sunset, and butter-yellow Golden Showers. The many benches beneath the pergola's shade are fragrant spots to contemplate the roses, the Bay, and beyond it, Mt. Tamalpais.

A fragrant canopy covers the pergola at Berkeley Rose Garden.

II Berkeley: Blake Garden

LOCATION: AT 70 RINCON ROAD IN KENSINGTON

Extending over 10 acres of elegantly planted woodlands and formal gardens in the Berkeley Hills, the historic Blake Garden recalls the halcyon days of 1920s garden estates. Anson Blake, a local businessman, and his wife Anita Day Symmes, both graduates of the University of California, Berkeley, developed the property. Designed by Walter Bliss, the Mediterranean-style Blake House was built in 1922, and the garden plan was designed a year later by Mabel Symmes, sister of Anita, who was trained at Berkeley as a landscape architect. Formal Italianate gardens were laid out on axis with the house. Italian stonemasons crafted stonework terraces and a staircase and grotto at the end of a reflecting pool. Encircling the house on the sloping land are woodland gardens and special collections of plants from Australia and the Mediterranean, many of them planted by Anita Blake, an avid gardener. In 1957, the Blakes deeded their garden to the university for instruction and research in landscape architecture. Since 1967, Blake House has been the official residence of the President of the University of California. The garden now contains as many as 1,100 species of plants from around the world, and serves as an instructional facility for the Department of Landscape Architecture and Environmental Planning at the university and other regional educational institutions. The formal gardens include a long water lily and koi-filled reflecting pool sur-

GARDEN OPEN: 8am–4:30pm Monday through Friday, closed on weekends and on university holidays, including New Year's Day, Independence Day, Thanksgiving, and Christmas Day

ADMISSION: Free

FURTHER INFORMATION FROM:
Blake Garden
Department of Landscape
Architecture
College of Environmental
Design
University of California
Berkeley 94720.
510.524.2449

NEARBY SIGHTS OF INTEREST:
University of California
Botanical Garden

ABOVE: *Formal and informal gardens flank the Mediterranean-style Blake House*

rounded by a shady garden room carpeted in grass and bordered with red-tinged hedges of *Syzgium paniculatum.* At the far end is the grotto, planted with white calla lilies, yellow primrose, and heavenly bamboo. Stone steps covered with wild strawberries lead up to a woodland path and drifts of iris and heuchera. The woodland path leads past deodara cedars and Canary Islands pines, white scillia and Chinese oak. A lawn area behind the house is rimmed with blue California wild lilacs (*Ceanothus*), and white wisteria climbs a wall. To the north of the house lies a redwood canyon that includes trees the Blakes propagated from burls they collected on family property at St. Helena, and dawn redwoods grown from seeds brought from China. To the west are xeric (or dry-land) gardens, including perennials such as Tuscan blue rosemary, red-hot pokers, and woody shrubs such as Fremontodendron with bright yellow flowers. A large area of Mediterranean plants includes lavenders and shrubby salvias. A wild-looking Australian garden to the southwest of the house is filled with acacias, eucalyptus, and provocative specimens such as echiums with eight-foot flower stalks. To the east of the house is a small pool surrounded by four parterre beds that brim with columbines, phlox, lobelia, coneflower, cosmos, and other colorful annuals and perennials. A shady lookout offers views across the San Francisco Bay to Mt. Tamalpais. A large vegetable and cutting garden near the greenhouse reminds us of the garden's ancillary role for decades in serving and complementing a gracious home.

GARDEN OPEN: 8:30am–5pm daily, closed New Year's, Thanksgiving, and Christmas Day
ADMISSION: Free (donations accepted)
FREE TOURS: Most Saturdays and Sundays at 2pm
FURTHER INFORMATION FROM:
Regional Parks Botanic Gardens
c/o Tilden Regional Park
Berkeley 94708.
510.841.8732
www.nativeplants.org

12 Berkeley: Regional Parks Botanic Garden

LOCATION: IN THE CENTER OF TILDEN REGIONAL PARK, AT THE INTERSECTION OF WILDCAT CANYON ROAD AND SOUTH PARK DRIVE

Located in Wildcat Canyon in the heart of the Berkeley Hills, the Regional Parks Botanic Garden is devoted to the collection, growth, display, and preservation of California native plants. Founded in 1940, it is a sanctuary for hundreds of the state's rare and endangered plants, and a wonderful place to view trees, shrubs, grasses, and flowers from plant communities around the state. The garden's temperate climate allows it to grow the state's diverse flora in ten acres that are divided into ten sections representing geographic regions. In this small canyon are plants from California's coastal bluffs, interior valleys, arid foothills, cool rain forests, alpine zones, and deserts. Plant labels are color-coded for each section. The overall design of the garden is unified by native rocks—many covered with interesting patterns and textures of lichens and mosses—that are used for walls, steps, a footbridge, and path edgings. The canyon walls offer east- and west-facing slopes, with Wildcat Creek dividing the garden on a north-south axis, ensuring that plants receive sun for at least part of the day, according to their natural preferences. Begun by the garden's founding director, James Roof, the collections include many California conifers, oaks, and manzanitas, as well as grasses, aquatic plants, and bulbs. The garden is maintained by the East Bay Regional Park District, with help from a nonprofit friends group. From the deck of the visitor center is a sweeping view of the garden and its repeated groupings of conifers and hardwoods. The view extends beyond to the surrounding hills, giving the impression of a much larger garden. As you wind down along the paved paths, you'll begin to appreciate the rich textures of this garden and the details of more delicate plants. Up close, you'll notice wonderful combinations, such as foothill penstemons, mariposa lilies, and creeping sage. Nootka reedgrass and foothill sedge mingle with yellow meadow foam (a rare and endangered plant from Point Reyes). This is truly a year-round garden: manzanitas, silk-tassels, and currants begin their display in January, followed by redbuds, bulbs, poppies, and lovely blue wild lilacs in early spring. A succession of flowers bloom through fall, when the vine maples, madrones, toyons, and willows transform the garden into a tapestry of reds, golds, bronzes, and silvers.

Rocky trails and native California trees abound at Berkeley's Regional Parks Botanic Gardens

13 El Cerrito: The Harland Hand Garden

LOCATION: NORTH OF BERKELEY IN A RESIDENTIAL SECTION OF EL CERRITO

On a half-acre of sloping land with dramatic views of the San Francisco Bay and the Golden Gate Bridge, Harland Hand created his garden over four decades with both an artist's eye and a devotion to displaying a broad palette of plants from around the world. A gifted garden designer and horticulturist, he viewed gardens as works of fine art. Inspired by the wildflowers in the woods of his native southern Minnesota and by the granite outcroppings of the Sierra, he composed a hillside rock garden of artfully sculpted concrete "rock" paths, benches, and pools interwoven with 2,000 varieties of interesting and rare plants. The richly planted garden, though beautiful year-round, is

GARDEN OPEN: Garden Conservancy Open Days or by appointment
ADMISSION: Donation requested
FURTHER INFORMATION FROM: Harland Hand Garden
825 Shevlin Drive
El Cerrito 94530.
510.525.9648

An artistically planted hillside rock garden at The Harland Hand Garden

especially so beginning in January when the large camellias bloom with azaleas and rhododendrons, and through the spring with a spectacular show of flowers and a white wisteria "tree" blooming in late April or May. An important element of his signature style was the use of extraordinary plants in ordinary ways and ordinary plants in extraordinary ways, such as combining orchids and succulents with roses and daisies. His background as an artist—he earned a master's degree in fine arts from UC Berkeley—informed his strong composition of textures and form, unusual color combinations, and contrasts of light and dark for dramatic impact. His background in science—he taught biology, physiology, and art at Oakland high schools for three decades—informed his knowledge of the plant world. After he retired in 1982, he devoted himself to his avocation, designing some two dozen gardens in the Bay Area before his death in 1998. His estate, overseen by his sister Lou Hand Schley, continues to fulfill his intention of preserving the garden to provide joy, inspiration, and instruction to horticulturists, designers, and others interested in gardens as art. Acknowledging the importance of this garden, the Garden Conservancy has selected it as a project worthy of preservation.

14 Oakland: Morcom Amphitheater of Roses

LOCATION: **700** JEAN STREET, ON CORNER OF GRAND AVENUE, NEAR DOWN-TOWN OAKLAND

GARDEN OPEN: Dawn to dusk daily

ADMISSION: Free

FURTHER INFORMATION FROM: Oakland Office of Parks and Recreation
1520 Lakeside Drive
Oakland 94612.
510.597.5039

The Morcom Amphitheater of Roses is a historic rose garden that looks much as it did when it was built in 1929. Named in honor of a former mayor of Oakland, the garden still features the same layout and many of the same roses. Part of a larger public park, the garden contains four acres of roses, surrounded by huge oak trees underplanted with ivy. From the main entrance on Grand Avenue to a central pool in the oval garden, roses bloom in luscious shades from deep orange to yellow to beige in symmetrical beds on either side of the main path. Surrounding the central pool are roses in deeper hues, such as the shocking pink Primadonna, a hybrid tea rose. On the left is the cascade garden planted with roses in delicate shades of white, pink, and beige. This garden of falling water and pastel blooms—and a clearing in the pines on a rise beyond it—are appropriately romantic settings for the many weddings that take place here from May through October. Along the perimeter of the cascade garden are climbing red and yellow roses. Leading from the central pool across from the entrance is a rose-bordered path known as the Mother's Walk, planted with floribundas, hybrid teas, and rose trees. (A Mother's Day ceremony held here each year since 1954 has honored outstanding local moms, who are given big bouquets of red roses). At the far end beyond the walk is the Florentine, a circular garden of heritage roses, including the tall, fragrant Lagerfeld rose in a lovely shade of lavender. This garden room is encircled by a stone wall with junipers on top that are decorated with lights throughout the year.

15 Walnut Creek: The Ruth Bancroft Garden

LOCATION: FROM I-580, FOLLOW YGNACIO VALLEY ROAD EAST TO BANCROFT ROAD, THEN TURN LEFT; GO 1 1/2 BLOCKS, TURN RIGHT AT **1400-1500** BANCROFT

GARDEN OPEN: By reservation only (call 925.210.9663)

ADMISSION: $5 adults

TOURS: Docent-led tours 9:30am Friday and Saturday, mid-April through mid-October, and 1pm from mid-April to July (1pm Saturday also from July through mid-October

FURTHER INFORMATION FROM: P.O. Box 30845
Walnut Creek 94598.
925.944.9352

Ruth Bancroft's two-and-a-half-acre garden is a canvas on which she paints strokes both bold and subtle. Noted for its exciting design and provocative combinations of diverse plants from around the world, the garden enjoys the hot dry summers of this sheltered inland valley. Working primarily with the dramatic forms of her beloved succulents, Ruth has created a work of fine art in the colors, textures, and patterns of foliage enhanced by curious and brilliant flowers. Some of the most beautiful are African aloes and their close relatives, the haworthias and gasterias. More than 100 species and hybrids of these, many produced in the garden, bloom with brilliant spikes of red, coral, orange, and yellow throughout the year, but particularly in late winter and spring. Tall stalks of white or cream flowers of agaves and yuccas appear in spring and summer. Meandering paths present an eclectic blend of exotic and native trees, shrubs, and flowering plants, from Australian bottle trees to Mexican blue palms to 300-year-old valley oaks. Columnar, barrel-like, wooly, and spiny, an extensive collection of cacti stand sentry in the garden. Pines, palo verde, and mesquite trees protect smaller, more tender plants from the sun. The garden was once part of a walnut orchard on the 400-acre ranch that her husband's grandfather, noted scholar of the western United States Hubert Howe Bancroft, owned from the 1880s. Ruth and her husband Phillip took over the ranch in the 1940s, and a decade later Ruth began to create the gardens surrounding the house and cultivate collections of potted succulents in greenhouses and shadehouses. In the late 1960s, Ruth began to develop her dry garden. Garden designer Lester Hawkins laid out the framework of mounded beds and winding paths in 1972. Ruth, who had been an architecture student at Berkeley, then arranged and planted her collection. The private garden was incorporated in 1993 as a nonprofit organization and is supported in part by the Garden Conservancy. At the age of 91, Ruth still worked in the garden daily, tending to some 2,000 of her "pets." When I asked whether gardening has kept her young, she replied with a wry smile that "it certainly keeps me busy."

A greenhouse for potted succulents at The Ruth Bancroft Garden

16 Menlo Park: Sunset Gardens

LOCATION: ON WILLOW ROAD, AT THE HEADQUARTERS OF SUNSET MAGAZINE

The Sunset Magazine headquarters in a residential area of
Menlo Park honor the work of two quintessential California
modern designers—architect Cliff May, father of the ranch-
style home, and Thomas Church, the dean of Western landscape architects. Opened to the public in 1952, the magazine's
corporate campus is an early example of environmental design,
with views of the trees and gardens as the focus of the low
sprawling ranch of adobe, plaster, and western woods with
patios and courtyards. The designs of the buildings and gardens express a seamless, indoor-outdoor lifestyle that was to
characterize the California style of the 1950s. The buildings
look out over seven acres of lawn, shrubs, trees, and flowers
that comprise one of Church's best preserved gardens. Views
through glass walls show a "back yard" ten times normal size,
with a central manicured lawn (once used as a putting green)
and a long curvilinear planting bed around the perimeter that
snakes along the banks of the San Francisquito Creek. Though
the plantings have changed, the bones of the garden remain—
mature oaks, redwoods, firs, dogwoods, and camellias. This is a
Technicolor garden, with a vast colorful display of Western
plants organized in geographic sections
from the Northwest to the California-
Mexico border. From primroses to poppies
to cacti, bright flowers provide plenty of
photo opportunities. Sunset also includes a
butterfly garden featuring buddleia,
heliotrope, penstemon, black-eyed Susans
and salvias, and a 3,200 square-foot area
for test plots of vegetables and flowers eval-
uated for coverage in the magazine. The
gardens represent a particular period and
lifestyle, and as such offer an intriguing
glimpse of the not-so-distant past.

GARDEN OPEN: 9am–4:30pm
Monday through Friday
ADMISSION: Free
FURTHER INFORMATION FROM:
Sunset Publishing
Corporation
80 Willow Road
Menlo Park 94025–3691.
650.321.3600
www.sunsetmagazine.com
NEARBY SIGHTS OF INTEREST:
Elizabeth F. Gamble Garden
Center, Filoli, Stanford
University

*Potted perennials on the
veranda of Sunset
headquarters*

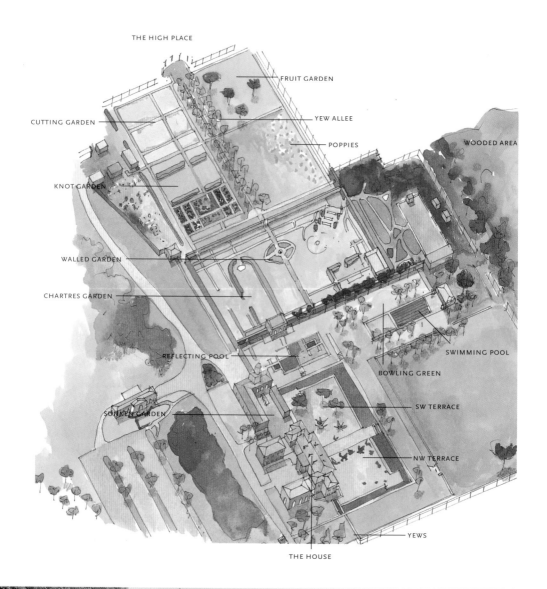

THE HIGH PLACE

FRUIT GARDEN

CUTTING GARDEN

YEW ALLEE

POPPIES

WOODED AREA

KNOT GARDEN

WALLED GARDEN

CHARTRES GARDEN

REFLECTING POOL

SWIMMING POOL

BOWLING GREEN

SUNKEN GARDEN

SW TERRACE

NW TERRACE

YEWS

THE HOUSE

17 Woodside: Filoli

LOCATION: ABOUT 25 MILES SOUTH OF SAN FRANCISCO JUST OFF HIGHWAY 280

A country lane leads through golden meadows to Filoli, cradled in a narrow valley of oaks, redwood, and madrone. One of America's finest historic garden estates, Filoli is an exquisite example of the elegant lines and proportions of the classic European estates united with an extraordinary natural setting. On a grand scale, the Filoli gardens are an early expression of the inside-outside lifestyle that became popular in California by the mid-twentieth century.

Filoli was born of three quintessential California circumstances: the earthquake of 1906, the Gold Rush, and the region's Mediterranean-like climate so conducive to gardening. William Bowers Bourn II and his wife Agnes built Filoli between 1915 and 1917 on the eastern slope of the Coast Range, south of San Francisco. The Bourns were prominent San Franciscans whose primary source of wealth was the Empire Mine, a gold mine in Grass Valley, California. Following the devastating earthquake and fire of 1906, many wealthy San Franciscans built estates on the Peninsula rather than rebuild in the city. Owner and president of the Spring Valley Water Company, William Bourn chose to build a country estate adjacent to the company's land at the south end of Crystal Springs Lake because it reminded him of the soft landscape and lakes of County Kerry, Ireland, where he owned Muckross, the great abbey estate in Killarney. He named his new estate Filoli, a composite of his credo, "fight for a just cause, love your fellow man, live a good life."

Bourn selected his longtime friend, architect Willis Polk, to design the 43-room, Georgian-style house. Bruce Porter, known for his interiors, murals, and stained glass and garden designs, planned the formal gardens. The house and gardens were designed as complementary units, with the north-south axis of the gardens echoing the lines of the house. Bourn loved the view of the hillside and lake, so the major portion of the gardens was sited so they wouldn't intrude upon the natural landscape. Inspired by European influences, the gardens comprise a series of "rooms" containing parterres, terraces, lawns, and pools arranged around a long north-south path. Over 200 Irish yews (*Taxa Baccata* 'Stricta') that had been grown from Muckross cuttings were transplanted to the gardens from the Bourn's summer home in Grass Valley. Isabella Worn supervised the planting of the gardens, continuing past the Bourns' deaths in 1936 until her own death at age 81 in 1950.

In 1937, William and Lurline Roth purchased Filoli, and for the next 38 years, Lurline greatly enriched the gardens with new plantings while preserving the original design. She intro-

GARDEN OPEN: Tuesday–Saturday from mid-February through November 1; call for hours

ADMISSION: $10

TOURS: Guided tours by appointment

FURTHER INFORMATION FROM: Friends of Filoli
86 Canada Road
Woodside 94062.
650.364.8300
www.filoli.org

OPPOSITE: *The colorful and complex Knot Garden at Filoli*

duced many shrubs and trees, including hundreds of camellia, rhododendrons, roses, magnolias, and greenhouse plants. Under her patronage, the gardens gained worldwide renown, and she was awarded honors such as the Distinguished Service Medal of the Garden Clubs of America for her achievements as a collector and propagator of plants. In 1975, the Roths gave the main residence and the gardens to the National Trust for Historic Preservation. The estate is now operated by the non-profit Filoli Center, with help from the Friends of Filoli. Today, the gardens display a rich and colorful palette of plants that includes beautiful ornamental trees and shrubs and thousands of flowers. In keeping with its own tradition, some 58,000 tulips and 16,000 narcissus are planted annually with the idea of incorporating new and better strains of old favorites.

In the center of the 654-acre estate is the historic house and 16 acres of enclosed gardens. The Filoli woodlands and the undeveloped watershed lands surrounding the core provide a magnificent backdrop for the gardens. Magnolias and Japanese maples greet visitors in the entry courtyard, and coast live oaks that are several hundred years old stand guard across from the north side of the house. Beautiful trees such as sculptured New Zealand tea trees and Chilean myrtles with fragrant white flowers and cinnamon-colored bark line the northwest and southwest terraces. White and lavender wisteria spill over various architectural features, such as the columned main entry and the terrace balustrades.

In the Sunken Garden, a marble-rimmed reflecting pool is skirted by brick walkways and border beds of spring bulbs, wildflowers such as blue columbine and orange wallflower, and annual and perennial flowers like pansies and delphinium. On the east side, in front of the Garden House, olive trees with

The Walled Garden

smooth gray bark are pleached (trimmed flat on top) and pruned so their open limbs and branches look like silvery filigree against a background of green yews. Fanlights and French doors flood the brick garden house with light for collections of potted flowers, trees, and ferns. The Garden House opens southward onto the Walled Garden, where the Chartres Cathedral Garden represents the celebrated stained-glass window with boxwood borders as the "leading" between beds of colorful annuals and roses. Behind the wall of the Cathedral Garden are two deciduous dawn redwoods, whose bronze needles in fall are lovely companions to the leaves of the copper beeches. At the south corner, the Wedding Place possesses the gardens' only diagonal lines: gently terraced grass steps that ascend to a fifteenth-century Venetian fountain of red marble. In the west corner, the Dutch Garden's mauve tulips and forget-me-nots fill beds within a maze-like series of boxwood hedges.

The path that leads through the center of the Walled Garden continues uphill through the yew allée to the High Place, which gives a long view of the north-south axis. To the west of the allée are a daffodil field and an orchard; to the east are a rose garden with more than 500 roses, a perennial border with espaliered fruit trees, a cutting garden, and the Knot Garden. The latter is one of Filoli's most intriguing places, because of the complex interweaving of rich colors and textures. Designed in the traditional style of English knot gardens of the sixteenth century with intricate, interlocking patterns and serpentine hedges, the Knot Garden is a sea of soft, fragrant, undulating herbs such as germander, lavender, and santolina and shrubs such as dwarf red Japanese barberry and myrtle. A long brick path leads from the rose garden southwest past a border of fragrant white iris to the Woodland Garden. Here, primroses, helebores, lilies of the valley, and star magnolias bloom in spring along stone-lined gravel paths. At the southwest end of the bowling green, bordered by London plane trees, two camperdown elms from Scotland nearly sweep the lawn with long gnarled branches, their spring leaves tinged with yellow. A lovely honey locust (*Gleditsia tricanthos* 'Sunburst'), exquisitely pruned olive trees, and Japanese maples gather near a pool pavilion, and double rows of tall dark Irish yews flank the long swimming pool. Returning west past the terraces adjacent to the house, you can appreciate how the gardens extended the lines and living space of the house into a series of outdoor rooms that pay homage to the classical garden styles of Europe while honoring the beauty of the California landscape.

The Georgian-style Filoli Center

GARDEN OPEN: Dawn to dusk
daily

ADMISSION: Free

TOURS: Docent-guided tours
are $3 per person, by reservation (minimum group of 8)

FURTHER INFORMATION FROM:

1431 Waverley Street
Palo Alto 94301.
650.329.1356
www.gamblegarden.org

Palo Alto: The Elizabeth F. Gamble Garden Center

LOCATION: OFF U.S. 101, EMBARCADERO WEST EXIT, AT THE CORNER OF
EMBARCADERO ROAD AND WAVERLEY STREET

During her lifetime, Elizabeth Frances Gamble lovingly tended her gardens and shared them with the community (she supplied flowers to a local hospital). She willed her two-and-a-third-acre estate to the city of Palo Alto when she died at age 92, in 1981, and the Garden Club of Palo Alto spearheaded a drive to preserve it as a garden center. It is now run by a non-profit horticultural foundation. Gamble's generous spirit lives on in the garden today. It is a popular spot for amateur and master gardeners and others to volunteer, take classes in the carriage house, or stroll in the gardens' quieter corners. The main house and carriage house were built in 1902 in a Colonial-revival style for Edwin Percy Gamble, a banker and son of James Gamble, co-founder of the Proctor & Gamble Company. The gardens were originally designed by San Franciscan Walter Hoff with many turn-of-the-century features. After Edwin's death, his daughter Elizabeth added a tea-house with its own garden, following a plan by Allan Reid. Today the gardens are divided in two parts: formal garden "rooms" surrounding the house, restored to reflect the original plan, and the working gardens. In the front of the house, Canary Island date palms, Irish yew, and magnolias set a period stage for the historic house. On the east side of the house, a cherry allée and grotto lead to a round garden of old roses. In the wisteria garden, mauve clouds of blooms enclose a lawn with clipped hedges around a fountain. Nearby is the tea house, and then a shady woodland garden with camellias, rhododendrons, snowball viburnums, and columbines. The working gardens are a huge tapestry, with a central gazebo and colorful, fragrant beds of Mediterranean herbs and annual and perennial flowers such as spiky delphiniums and foxglove. There are artfully planted demonstration beds, many with new varieties of plants that grow well in the region or offer solutions to gardening problems, such as fruit trees espaliered to save space and raised planting beds, accessible to visitors in wheelchairs. Near the center is a large border of iris—Elizabeth Gamble's favorite flower—that includes a gorgeous periwinkle blue variety that bears her name. Bees and butterflies by the dozens alight on the flowers, and Anna's hummingbirds chatter throughout the garden, diving for the salvia beds' bursts of scarlet and purple flowers.

Delphinium and foxglove surround the gazebo.

19 Saratoga: Hakone Gardens

LOCATION: AT **21000** BIG BASIN WAY

In 1916, San Francisco art patrons Oliver and Isabel Stine purchased 16 acres of Saratoga hillside to build a summer retreat for family and friends. Inspired by displays at the 1915 Pan-Pacific Exposition, Isabel Stine traveled to Japan to gather ideas. Inspired especially by the Fuji-Hakone National Park, she returned home to begin her own Hakone Gardens. In 1918, she retained architect Tsunematsu Shintani to design the upper moon viewing house, and landscape gardener Naoharu Aihara to design the gardens. In 1932, ownership of the gardens passed to prominent East Bay financier Major C.L.Tilden, who added the main gate. In 1966, the city of Saratoga purchased the gardens to keep them from being subdivided and developed. The city hired Tanso Ishihara, a landscape gardener trained in Kyoto, to begin restoring the gardens. After his death, his student, Jack Tomlinson, worked with Mrs. Ishihara to maintain the gardens' beauty and authenticity. Four gardens comprise a quiet place that captures the essence of Japanese garden style through the harmonious placement of plants, stones, and water. The hill and pond garden, perfect for strolling, is the heart of Hakone. Paths wind around the pond's north slope, past a waterfall and plantings of azaleas, camellias, ferns, ivy, and delicate Japanese maples. The path continues to an island and then over an arched footbridge. Huge turtles and koi swim near a wisteria-covered pavilion that pro-

GARDEN OPEN: 10am–5pm Monday–Friday, 11am–5pm Saturday, Sunday, and holidays, closed New Year's Day and Christmas Day
ADMISSION: $5 for parking
FURTHER INFORMATION FROM:
Hakone Foundation
P.O. Box 2324
Saratoga 95070.
408.741.4994
www.hakone.com
NEARBY SIGHTS OF INTEREST:
Villa Montalvo

ABOVE: *The heart of Hakone: hill and pond garden*

vides a place to rest and view artful plant combinations such as
deep rose peonies, horsetail, and yellow bog iris. The tranquil
tea garden path over moss and stones leads guests to the tea
house entrance (a tea ceremony is held the first Thursday of
every month between 1pm and 4pm, by reservation). The Zen
garden is a dry garden of raked gravel and lichen-covered rocks
that represent water and islands. Accents include a shrine
lantern, a black pine tree, and tiny succulent plants. Enclosed
by a low bamboo fence, it is meant for meditative viewing and
is never entered. The *Kizuna–en* is a bamboo garden that represents the close friendship between Saratoga and its sister
city, Muko–shi, near Kyoto. Maintained by the Japan Bamboo
Society of Saratoga, it is a highly symbolic garden, with large
stones representing the city councils of both cities and white
gravel suggesting the Pacific Ocean. Closed in the spring to
encourage and protect new growth, it displays 18 kinds of bamboo, from giant timber bamboo to the playfully named
Buddha's belly variety.

20 ## Saratoga: Villa Montalvo

LOCATION: ON MONTALVO ROAD, OFF HIGHWAY 9/SARATOGA-LOS GATOS
ROAD

GARDEN OPEN: 8am–5pm
Monday–Friday, 9am–5pm
Saturday and Sunday
ADMISSION: Free
FURTHER INFORMATION FROM:
15400 Montalvo Road
PO Box 158
Saratoga 95071–0158.
408.961.5800
www.villamontalvo.org

Villa Montalvo, a historic estate for the arts, ushers visitors to
another time and place—perhaps an Italian country estate at
the turn of the last century. Villa Montalvo's 175 lovely acres
combine the peaceful ambiance of a park with the vitality of
the arts—celebrated in the formal gardens that surround the
villa, on the great lawn, in an octagonal carriage house theater,
and in a garden amphitheater. The estate was built in 1912 by
James Duval Phelan, a passionate Californian who served as
San Francisco's progressive mayor from 1897 to 1903, and
would later become the state's first popularly elected U.S.
Senator. Gracing a hillside that overlooks the southern tip of
San Francisco Bay and Silicon Valley, the Mediterranean-style
villa was Phelan's favorite home and a center for the arts, poli-
tics, and society life in Northern California. When he died in
1930, Phelan wished his estate to be used as a public park "for
the development of art, literature, music, and architecture."
Villa Montalvo is home to the oldest artist residency program
on the West Coast, and regularly presents musical perfor-
mances. Wrapping the house, a veranda overlooks the luxurious expanse of front lawn, embellished on the perimeter with
ancient-looking urns and date palms, madrone, and sweet olive
trees. Leading from the lawn are nature trails that wind
through three miles of wooded slopes. From the villa's front
steps, a long vista sweeps past elaborate wrought-iron gates at
the end of the lawn to the Meditation Garden and Love Temple

Garden beyond, both quiet, evocative spots that suggest secrecy. Set into a slope behind the villa are several charming gardens. One is the Spanish courtyard with manicured shrubbery and circulating fountains sloping down from the villa's main gallery. An oval garden between the villa and the garden theater features a pavilion, clipped boxwood hedges, and a curved, wisteria-draped pergola. Next to it are perennial gardens with lily of the Nile, lavender, snow-in-summer, and golden lilies. Allusions to the classical world abound throughout the garden in the form of marble statues, decorative stone benches, and an Egyptian obelisk and sphynx. Walking around the grounds late on a summer's day, when the light softened in the gardens, I was inspired to offer James Phelan silent thanks for a place of such beauty and serenity.

Boxwood hedges and a wisteria-draped pergola define the oval garden at Villa Montalvo

21 Santa Cruz: University of California at Santa Cruz Arboretum

LOCATION: HIGH STREET (EMPIRE GRADE), BETWEEN EAST AND WEST ENTRANCES TO CAMPUS

GARDEN OPEN: 9am–5pm daily, closed Thanksgiving and Christmas Day
ADMISSION: Free (donations appreciated)
FURTHER INFORMATION FROM:
Arboretum
University of California
Santa Cruz 95064.
831.427.2998
www2.ucsc.edu/arboretum/

Rolling over meadows and bluffs with spectacular vistas of Monterey Bay and the Pacific Ocean, the University of California at Santa Cruz Arboretum offers both a sweeping panorama and exquisite details in the plants that grow here from all over the world. Started in 1964 with a gift of 90 species of eucalyptus trees, the 130-acre arboretum now boasts the largest collection of Australian plants outside their native country, with more than 2,000 varieties, including brilliantly colored grevilleas, banksias, acacias, and waratahs. One of the richest places for horticulture on the planet, Australia is home to a wide range of fascinating plants. As in California, plants may experience long periods of drought, followed by sudden heavy rains, both of which make pollination difficult. Consequently, the most noticeable and alluring plants get pollinated, which explains the scarlet flowering gum, the spiky red and gold flowers of Silver Princess eucalyptus, and the huge, deep rose flower heads of waratahs (*Telopea speciosissima*), an evergreen shrub. Nearly 50 species of banksias grow here, from trees to small, fernlike plants with inflorescences that emerge from the ground. Some Australian plant or other will be blooming year-round, though the greatest show is from January

Protea obtusifolia at the UC Santa Cruz Arboretum

through April. Paths take you through grasslands and riparian areas to 45 acres of plant communities from New Zealand, Africa, South America, and California. The New Zealand collection displays bizarre plants—some with wiry zigzag branchlets and absurdly small leaves that may have evolved as defenses against giant moas, the ancient flightless birds with devastating beaks that grazed New Zealand for millions of years. The South African plants include a lovely collection of Cape heaths, many with bell-like flowers. Some of the showiest South African plants are in the Protea family, such as king proteas with blooms nearly a foot in diameter, magnificent white or reddish-pink Queen proteas from high on the mountainsides, pink, orange, and red pincushions, and long showing leucadendrons, some of which are silvery blue and 30 feet tall. Scarlet-throated Anna's hummingbirds and mourning cloak butterflies flock to the cacti, succulents, and wildflowers in the California section. Other garden areas include one of the world's largest collections of conifers and another for drought-tolerant aromatic herbs and shrubs such as mints, lavenders, thymes, and oreganos. The arboretum is a fun place for families; children delight in the maze of paths and the abundant wildlife, and picnic tables and handmade benches tucked away throughout the grounds offer places to relax with the views.

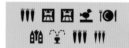

GARDEN OPEN: 8am–5pm daily, closed Thanksgiving, Christmas, and New Year's Day
ADMISSION: $14 adult, $8 ages 6–12, children under 6 free
TOURS: Call for ticket reservations, 1.800.444.4445
FURTHER INFORMATION FROM: 750 Hearst Castle Road San Simeon 93452. 805.927.2020 www.hearstcastle.org

22 San Simeon: Hearst San Simeon State Historical Monument

LOCATION: ON HIGHWAY 1 ACROSS FROM OLD TOWN SAN SIMEON

A National Historic Landmark, Hearst Castle was the home of William Randolph Hearst, the publishing and film magnate. His father George, a wealthy miner, had purchased 40,000 acres of ranchland in 1865, and by the time William inherited it in 1919, the ranch encompassed 250,000 acres. William Hearst hired famed San Francisco architect Julia Morgan to collaborate on a house and gardens on a spot he called *la cuesta encantada,* or "the enchanted hill." By 1947, the estate had grown to 165 rooms and 127 acres of gardens with terraces, staircases, pools, and fountains. Hearst collaborated with his architect, Julia Morgan, to create a garden design in harmony with the estate's Mediterranean revival-style buildings and inspired by the great Italian and Spanish gardens of Europe. They capitalized on the gardens' magnificent setting, with panoramic views of mountains, coastline, and ocean, and used the hilltop's native coastal live oaks and bay trees in their design. They added other large trees such as Italian cypress and Mexican fan palms to help integrate the scale of the towering main house, La Casa Grande, with the smaller scale of the surrounding gardens and guesthouses. The details of the garden design recall the rich history of Moorish gardens, with glazed, colored ceramic tiles on walls and fountain bases. Geometric flower beds outlined with clipped hedges of boxwood and myrtle mimicked the parterres of French and Italian gardens, and classical sculpture fragments, fountains, and pergolas lent the character of Italian Renaissance gardens. Hearst wanted a garden with a profusion of blooms, so hundreds of thousands of annuals, perennials, and bulbs were planted throughout the year—bougainvillea, tulips, hyacinths, gladiolas, lilies, dahlias, asters, geraniums, lantana, petunias, pansies, hollyhocks, marigolds, and carnations. Hearst's longtime head gardener, Norman Rotanzi, oversaw the diverse plant palette after Hearst's death in 1951 (and after the property was deeded to the state in 1957) until his own death in 1992. Today the gardens are much as they were in Hearst's era. The formal gardens showcase 300 varieties of annuals, perennials, and tropical plants, as well as more than 1,000 rose bushes of about 80 different cultivars (though most are modern hybrids that did not exist in Hearst's day). The Esplanade exemplifies the elegantly clipped trees and flowering shrubs that provided texture and color—Victorian box, snowball viburnums, veronica, fuchsias, Grecian bay, myrtle, Chinese lantern, and orange and tangerine trees that have been pleached or pruned like a hedge on top. Near the marble-lined Neptune pool, Roman temple façade, and colonnades are foxgloves, lily of the Nile, cannas, deep red Chrysler Imperial hybrid tea roses, and Italian cypress. Along the south terrace are oleanders, flowering gum, pomegranate hedges, and hibiscus. The grand effect of the gardens harmonizing with the architecture and surrounding landscape is a rare and splendid treat.

La Casa Grande, William Randolph Hearst's palatial former home

GARDEN OPEN: 9am–5pm
Monday through Friday,
Saturday and Sunday until
6pm, March through
October; 9am–4pm Monday
through Friday, Saturday and
Sunday until 5pm, November
through February

ADMISSION: $5 adults, $3
seniors and teenagers, $1
ages 5–12, children under 5
free

FURTHER INFORMATION FROM:
1212 Mission Canyon Road
Santa Barbara 93105.
805.682.4726
www.sbbg.org

NEARBY SIGHTS OF INTEREST:
Ganna Walska Lotusland,
Santa Barbara Mission,
Museum of Natural History

23 Santa Barbara: Santa Barbara Botanic Garden

LOCATION: FROM DOWNTOWN SANTA BARBARA, TAKE LOS OLIVOS ROAD, TURN RIGHT ON FOOTHILL ROAD (RT. 192), THEN ONE MILE UP MISSION CANYON ROAD

A wildflower palette of purple lupines, blue-eyed grass, white meadow foam, and orange California poppies in the meadow of the Santa Barbara Botanic Garden inspires the artist in all of us. Elsewhere in the garden, wild blue lilacs (*Ceanothus*) bloom in early spring, followed by iris, monkeyflower, penstemon, and fragrant sage. By summer, the garden's woodland trail and redwood forest offer a cool retreat from the coastal fog and inland heat. Autumn's fuchsias, roses, sycamores, and big-leaf maples brighten the woodlands and canyons linked by five-and-a-half-miles of trail; in winter, toyons burst with red berries, manzanitas bloom, and early wildflowers carpet the ground. Established in 1926 by Anna Blaksley Bliss as a memorial to her father, the garden began as a place to research and display plants native to the Pacific slope, and was administered by the Santa Barbara Museum of Natural History. Over the years, it expanded to 65 acres, narrowed its focus to California native flora, and became a nonprofit institution independent of the museum. Today, more than 1,000 kinds of native flowers, shrubs, and trees grow here, with more than 86,000 specimens of native plants housed in the herbarium. Included among these are many rare and elusive plants that are indigenous to the Channel Islands, visible to the south of the garden from strategically placed viewpoints, and from the slopes of the Santa Ynez Mountains looming to the north. A desert garden near the entrance exhibits cacti, agaves, jojoba, and silvery-gray brittlebrush, whose stems produce fragrant resin the local Indians chewed or burned as incense in churches. A home demonstration garden displays water-conserving perennials and ground covers for southern California gardens. Trails lead to a half-dozen diverse sections, such as an arroyo, with conifers, giant sequoias, and Port Orford cedars, and the towering coast redwood grove, underplanted with ferns, redwood sorrel, and wild ginger. From the stone overlooks in the meadow garden, you can see down a sharp cliff to Mission Creek and the dam that the Indians built for the Franciscan padres in the early 1800s. The woodland trail passes through the redwood grove and crosses the creek over the dam-bridge. The canyon trail explores the riparian oak woodland along the creek, and leads to the Easton-Aqueduct trail, where you may see portions of the historic aqueduct system the Indians built to direct water to the Mission. The trails are rated easy to moderate, and are depicted on an excellent color map available at the information kiosk near the entrance.

24 Santa Barbara: Ganna Walska Lotusland

LOCATION: **695** ASHLEY ROAD

Noted for its remarkable and often bizarrely shaped botanical treasures, the 37-acre Ganna Walska Lotusland leads garden lovers on an aesthetic and scientific adventure that is every bit as colorful and dramatic as the garden's eponymous creator. Ganna Walska, a Polish-born opera star—already married six times to men of influence and fortune—focused her energy on her gardens when she purchased Lotusland in 1941. In the 1880s, pioneer nurseryman R. Kinton Stevens had planted Chilean wine palms, sacred Indian lotus, and other subtropical plants. Subsequent owners Mr. and Mrs. E. Palmer Gavit commissioned the design of the original gardens, which included a formal parterre garden, hedged allées, and a pool and fountain. The celebrated local architect George Washington Smith, who designed the swimming pool, bathhouse, and pink perimeter wall, also remodeled their 1919 California Spanish-style home. Madame, as Walska was known, added a pavilion, another pool (turning the old one into a lotus garden), a small theater of clipped Monterey cypress, and a topiary garden. As she continued to modify Lotusland, she consulted two of Santa Barbara's finest landscape architects, Lockwood de Forest and Ralph T. Stevens (the son of R. Kinton Stevens). The gardens are much as they were when she created them. Her signature style includes whimsical, flamboyant, and extravagant uses of plants and garden ornaments. Grotesque stone dwarfs brought from her French estate populate the garden. Thickly planted dragon trees guard the doorway to the main house, while next to it stand equally forbidding *Euphorbia ingens* from southeast Africa, whose trunks rise 30 feet and tumble back to earth, coiling and writhing along the ground like snakes among the barrel cactus. In the fescue-carpeted blue garden, irregular chunks of turquoise slag glass border the paths like the huge jewels Madame favored. She also loved masses of plants. Legend has it that, anticipating a visit from the Palm Society, she ordered 100 additional palms trucked in and planted at the last minute. In the aloe garden, more than 130 species— many with spiky and fiery blooms—reach skyward with thousands of sword-like leaves. In these and other areas—a serene Japanese garden, a fern garden with huge staghorn specimens suspended from trees, a collection of scarlet and chartreuse bromeliads, a cactus garden with old-man cacti, covered with white "hair," and appearing to fire-walk on red-and-black lava

GARDEN OPEN: Mid-February–mid-November, for 2 hour walking tours, by advance reservation

ADMISSION: $10 adults (children under 10 not permitted)

FURTHER INFORMATION FROM: Ganna Walska Lotusland Foundation
695 Ashley Road
Santa Barbara 93108.
805.969.3767
www.lotusland.org

NEARBY SIGHTS OF INTEREST: Santa Barbara Botanic Garden, Santa Barbara Mission

Sacred Indian lotus plants for which the garden is named

stones—her love of plants is paramount. Her final creation (before her death at 100 in 1984) was the cycad garden. Here, 400 of these prehistoric, stiff-fronded plants (including three South American *Encephalartos woodii*, which no longer exist in the wild) rise like monolithic sculptures on a lawn and around a pond. Opened to the public in 1993, the garden by county law limits visitors to 13,500 a year, admitted in small, docent-led groups and by reservation only.

25 Beverly Hills: Virginia Robinson Gardens

LOCATION: CRESCENT DRIVE AND ELDON WAY

GARDEN OPEN: Guided walking tours by appointment only
ADMISSION: $7 adults, $4 seniors and students, $2 children
TOURS: 10am and 1pm Tuesday through Thursday, 10am Friday
FURTHER INFORMATION FROM:
1008 Eldon Way
Beverly Hills 90210.
310.276.5367

Southern California in the early twentieth century was replete with estate gardens inspired by the exotic gardens of Spain, Italy, and Portugal. The region's climate invited the use of Mediterranean plants and classic formal garden designs on estates such as Virginia and Harry Robinson's. Returning from an extended three-year honeymoon to Europe and Asia, the Robinsons (of the J.W. Robinson department store empire) built a beaux arts-style home designed by Virginia's father, Nathaniel Dryden, on 15 acres at the highest spot in what is now known as Beverly Hills. Like their neighbors, they planned exotic gardens to surround the house; the results, however, were proof of their extraordinary interest in plants and garden design. Traveling often to Europe, they returned with seeds of rare and exotic plants. In 1918, they built an Italian Renaissance-style garden on a four-acre slope west of the main house. They created a series of patio gardens with small fountains and pools as part of an intricate water system that flowed down the terraced hillside. In 1921, at the suggestion of landscape architect Charles Gibbs Adams, Virginia Robinson planted three acres of palms to the east of the main house. After her husband's death in 1932, she continued to expand the gardens, planting rare tropical and subtropical plants such as ear pod trees, monkey hand trees, and a large collection of Chamaedorea palms. Just short of her 100th birthday in 1977, Virginia died, leaving her home and gardens to Los Angeles County to be preserved as an historical site. Opened to the public in 1981, the gardens are managed by the county, with support from the Friends of the Robinson Gardens. Today, the Virginia Robinson Gardens, listed on the National Register of Historic Places, span six hillside acres and five distinct gardens. The Italian terrace garden connects visitors via brick paths with pools, fountains, and views of citrus terraces and magnolias, camellias, gardenias, clivias, and azaleas. The formal mall offers perennial borders and specimen cycads in the lawn. The Renaissance-revival pool pavilion, modeled after the famous Villa Pisani in Italy, is embellished with mosaic tile wainscoting around the pool and sgraffito ornamentation on the Roman arches. A rose garden and kitchen garden support the rarified life of a manor home, and the tropical palm garden blooms with gingers, bananas, and fragrant plumeria. Towering over this cool, dense glade are many of the original palms, including Mediterranean fan palms, windmill palms, and Australian king palms that comprise the largest collection of that species in the continental United States.

26 Los Angeles: Mildred E. Mathias Botanical Garden

LOCATION: ON THE SOUTHEAST CORNER OF THE UCLA CAMPUS, ON TIVERTON AVENUE

A visit to the Mildred E. Mathias Botanical Garden on the campus of UCLA is something like a trip to the tropics. The garden's seven acres are frost-free, and thus tropical and subtropical plants are perfectly happy here outdoors. Among the 4,000 species in 275 plant families are special collections of ferns, palms, eucalyptus, and figs—the latter two collections dating to the early years of the garden, before they became widely planted throughout the Los Angeles region. The garden was started as an academic laboratory in 1930, about the time the university moved to Westwood, along an arroyo on the east side of the campus where native willows grew along the creek bed and coastal sage scrub studded the dry hills. The first gardener, George C. Groenewegen, obtained plants largely by donation from a U.S. Department of Agriculture plant introduction site and from other botanical gardens such as The Huntington. By 1947, the garden contained about 1,500 species and varieties of plants. In 1979, it was named in honor of botanist Dr. Mildred E. Mathias, director from 1956 to 1974. Plants are arranged by geographic, taxonomic, or cultural needs to show students and visitors characteristics of relatedness. They are also organized according to themes, such as desert plants, aquatic plants, Mediterranean-climate shrubs, and native Hawaiian plants. The cycad collection displays these large gymnosperms that were common when dinosaurs roamed the earth. The bromeliads, members of the pineapple family with beautiful water-capturing leaves and cone-shaped flowers, lend an especially tropical atmosphere, and the lily alliance, ranging from trees to vines to rosette plants with

GARDEN OPEN: 8am–5pm Monday–Friday (winter closing 4pm), 8am–4pm Saturday and Sunday, closed university holidays
ADMISSION: Free
FURTHER INFORMATION FROM: University of California
405 Hilgard Avenue
Los Angeles 90024-1606.
310.825.1260 or 310.206.6707 for group tours
www.lifesci.ucla.edu/botgard

The arid garden at Mildred E. Mathias Botanical Garden

showy flowers, display the diversity of this plant family. A walking tour (included in a brochure available at the information kiosk on Tiverton Avenue) begins at the north entrance. It points out such massive specimens as a Torrey pine, an endangered species resistant to urban smog, a dawn redwood, perhaps the tallest in North America, and two rose gums (*Eucalyptus grandis*), natives of the rain forest of Queensland, Australia.

27 La Cañada Flintridge: Descanso Gardens

LOCATION: OFF 210 FREEWAY AND FOOTHILL BOULEVARD

GARDEN OPEN: 9–4:30 daily, except Christmas Day
ADMISSION: $5, $3 seniors and students, $1 ages 5–12, under 5 free
FURTHER INFORMATION FROM:
1418 Descanso Drive
La Canada Flintridge 91011.
818.952.4401
www.descanso.com
NEARBY SIGHTS OF INTEREST:
The Huntington, The Arboretum of Los Angeles County, Norton Simon Museum

The teahouse at Descanso, surrounded by native trees and rhododenron

Nestled in a natural bowl in the San Rafael Hills, the Descanso Gardens are a peaceful refuge amidst the urban development of Los Angeles. The 160-acre gardens are renowned for its camellia collection—60,000 plants, perhaps the world's largest—planted in an oak forest and surrounded by chaparral. E. Manchester Boddy, a successful businessman who published the old *Los Angeles Daily News*, created the gardens in 1936. Boddy fell in love with the site, planting his first dozen camellia in 1936. He named it Rancho del Descanso ("where I rest") and in 1938 built a 22-room mansion, later purchasing an additional 280 acres north of the property for a watershed to irrigate his growing commercial camellia nursery. In 1941, he hired J. Howard Asper, a world-famous camellia expert. Together, they succeeded in popularizing camellia, especially for use in corsages. At its peak, Rancho del Descanso had 600,000 camellia plants. Boddy's interests expanded to roses, and he hired rose breeder Dr. Walter E. Lammerts to establish a five-acre rose history garden (Lammerts also developed hybrid native lilacs for the garden). The business thrived until 1953, when Boddy sold the property to the County of Los Angeles. By 1957, however, the county considered selling the property, and a group of 25 local residents formed the nonprofit Descanso Gardens Guild to preserve the gardens. Since then, the guild, which manages the gardens, has created a Japanese teahouse and gardens, and a lake and bird sanctuary. Today, the gardens are filled with the sounds of cascading waterfalls and birdsong (the local Audubon Society conducts bird tours at 8am the second and fourth Sundays of the month). In addition to the camellia forests, there are 80 acres of perennial beds, thousands of tulips and other spring-flowering bulbs, a seven-and-a-half-acre native plant area, and a lilac grove featuring Lavender Lady and other Descanso hybrids. A refurbished iris garden contains more than 1,500 varieties of bearded iris. The original rose garden, developed into the International Rosarium, displaying 4,000 roses, includes species, antique, and modern roses, as well as thousands of flowering trees, shrubs, and flowers. The Rosarium is divided into 20 themed "rooms," such as the Mission Garden and the Children's Secret Garden (children also enjoy riding on the garden's "enchanted railroad"). Paths are wheelchair accessible, and a tram transports visitors to the major garden areas.

Rose Pavillion in the International Rosarium

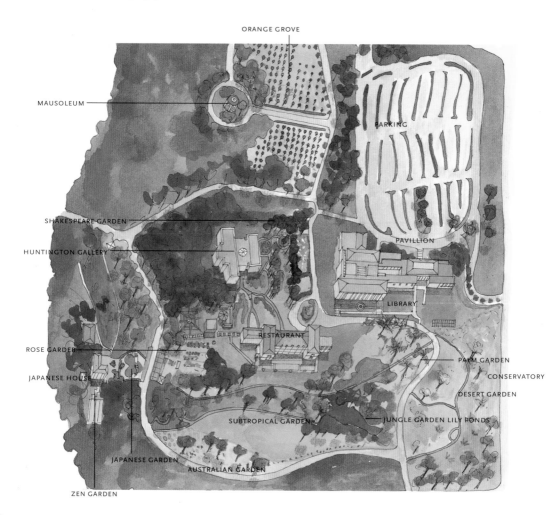

ORANGE GROVE

MAUSOLEUM

PARKING

SHAKESPEARE GARDEN

PAVILLION

HUNTINGTON GALLERY

LIBRARY

RESTAURANT

ROSE GARDEB

PALM GARDEN

JAPANESE HOUSE

CONSERVATORY

DESERT GARDEN

SUBTROPICAL GARDEN

JUNGLE GARDEN LILY PONDS

JAPANESE GARDEN

AUSTRALIAN GARDEN

ZEN GARDEN

28 San Marino: The Huntington

LOCATION: ADJACENT TO PASADENA; NEAREST MAJOR CROSS STREETS ARE
ALLEN AVENUE/CALIFORNIA BOULEVARD (NORTH) OR HUNTINGTON
DRIVE/SIERRA MADRE BOULEVARD (SOUTH).

Henry E. Huntington, a railroad tycoon and real estate developer from the East Coast who came to California in the
1890s,became enamored of the beauty (and business possibilities) of the San Gabriel Valley, and bought the 600-acre San
Marino Ranch in 1903. With the help of a young landscape gardener, William Hertrich, he began transforming the working
ranch with commercial crops of citrus, peaches, nuts, grains,
and avocados into a grand estate that showcased his growing
collection of diverse botanical specimens. Beginning with the
lily ponds, palm garden, and the desert collection, they developed a series of formal and informal garden spaces connected
by rolling lawns and vistas.

Plants were not Henry Huntington's only passion. He collected books and developed an interest in art, influenced largely
by Arabella Duval Huntington. She was the widow of his uncle
Collis, with whom Huntington had managed the Southern
Pacific and Central Pacific railroads. Henry and Arabella married in 1913, when they were both in their 60s (his first marriage had ended in divorce), and moved into the beaux arts-style
mansion built in 1911 by Los Angeles architects Myron Hunt
and Elmer Grey. Together Henry and Arabella amassed magnificent collections of rare books and manuscripts, eighteenth
and nineteenth-century British and French art, and American
art from the eighteenth to the early twentieth century.
Huntington planned carefully for his collections; in 1919 he set
up a deed of trust to preserve them and establish a research
institution for scholars. In 1928, a year after his death, his property and collections were transferred to a nonprofit trust, which
continues to own and operate The Huntington Library, its art
collections, and the gardens.

The gardens cover 150 acres of the 207-acre grounds in a
park-like landscape with 15 distinct garden areas (self-guided
tour brochures are available in the entrance pavilion). More
than 14,000 different kinds of plants are displayed, including
10,000 different species in the 12-acre desert garden alone.
William Hertrich's idea for a desert garden initially met with
opposition from Huntington, who had a painful encounter
with cacti decades earlier while supervising railroad construction in Arizona. But Hertrich eventually won over his boss and
began the garden in 1905. Today, it contains one of the world's
largest collections of cacti and succulents, including epiphytic
cacti from the Latin American tropics, Crown of Thorns
(*Euphorbia milii* var. *splendens*) from Madagascar, and black aeo-
nium from North Africa, as well as many agaves, aloes, yuccas,

RECORDED DIRECTIONS:
626.405.2274
GARDEN OPEN: 12–4:30pm
Tuesday–Friday,
(10:30am–4:30pm Memorial
Day through Labor Day),
10:30am–4:30pm Saturday
and Sunday, closed
Mondays and major holidays
ADMISSION: $8.50 adults, $8
seniors, $6 students 12 and
older, children under 12 free,
free first Thursday of month
TOURS: Docent-led tours at
1pm and as posted
FURTHER INFORMATION FROM:
1151 Oxford Road
San Marino 91108.
626.405.2100
www.huntington.org

OPPOSITE: *Huntington
Gallery*

TOP: *Desert Garden*
MIDDLE: *North Vista
Fountain*
BOTTOM: *Rose Garden*

and puyas. They also began the palm garden in 1905, where today, there are more
than 200 species of the towering trees,
including the endangered Chilean wine
palm (*Jubaea chilensis*) and California's
only native palm, *Washingtonia filifera*.
Extending from the Huntington Gallery
(formerly the Huntingtons' home) is one of
the gardens' most memorable spots: the
north vista. Tall columns of fountain palms
and seventeenth-century statues from
Padua, Italy, flank the lawn that leads to an
Italian Renaissance stone fountain and
frame a view of the San Gabriel Mountains.
Surrounding the north vista is the camellia
garden, containing 1,200 cultivars of the
three principal species of camellia—sasan-
qua, japonica, and reticulata (notice in particular a newer cultivar: the large, pink,
semi-double Henry E. Huntington). A second camellia garden is located north of the
Japanese garden. Just north of the gallery is
the Shakespeare garden, planted with
herbs and flowers mentioned in the bard's
plays, such as violets, rosemary, pomegranate, poppies, and pansies. The White Rose
of York and the Red Rose of Lancaster,
among the oldest cultivated roses, represent the opposing factions in the fifteenth-
century War of the Roses.

A rose arbor leads to the three-acre
rose garden, established in 1908, which
consists of nearly 1,500 cultivars. It is
arranged historically so that you may view
(and smell) the history of the rose from the
early European blooms of the Middle Ages
and Renaissance, to tea and China roses
introduced to Europe around 1800, to classic hybrid teas, floribundas, polyanthas,
and miniature roses. Entrance pathways
wind to an eighteenth-century French
stone *tempietto* containing *Love, the Captive
of Youth*, a statue of Cupid and a fair
maiden. The *tempietto* is encircled by a bed
of French lace roses, a romantic theme that
continues through the garden with blooms
such as Secret Love, Careless Love, and
Sweet Surrender. The rose garden was
originally created for the private enjoyment
of Henry and Arabella, and was a source

for the large, elaborate floral arrangements that the near-sighted Arabella favored. Household records indicate some 30,000 flowers were used in floral arrangements one year—and 9,700 of them were roses. (To prolong your enjoyment of this romantic spot, consider having English tea in the rose garden's tearoom.)

The Japanese garden, established in 1912, is said to have been a gift from Henry to Arabella. She was skeptical about the attractions of Southern California as a new permanent home, and Henry hoped to appease her with an exotic pleasure garden, designed in a fashionable Oriental motif with koi ponds, a moon bridge, votive stones, and a nineteenth-century Japanese house with traditional furnishings. Constructed in what had been a rugged gorge filled with trees, wild grape vines, and poison oak, the Japanese Garden required the removal of hundreds of truckloads of dirt and gravel from an old dam, regrading and building terraces, and extensive landscaping. Today, it is serene and especially lovely during the springtime blooms of wisteria, azaleas, and peach, apricot, and cherry trees. A zigzag bridge leads to a Zen garden, a quiet place for contemplation with a dry sand and rock garden raked to represent a flowing stream. Beyond is a smaller court with a collection of bonsai, or dwarfed trees and plants.

South and east of the art gallery are a series of special collections. The Australian garden features 150 species of eucalyptus, including *Eucalyptus macrocarpa*, a low-spreading shrub with silvery blue-green leaves and large red flowers, as well as kangaroo paws (*Anigozanthos*), acacias, bottle brushes, cycads, and melaleucas. Plants from the Mediterranean climates of South Africa, South America, the Canary Islands, Southeast Asia, and Mexico such as cassias, bauhinias, and jacarandas grow in the subtropical garden. And orchids, bamboo, and ferns create a lush tropical forest in the jungle garden, which also features a waterfall, lily ponds and a rich understory of blooms with gingers, calla lilies, bromeliads, and sacred Indian lotus.

Rebutia krainziana, *a Bolivian cactus*

GARDEN OPEN: 9am–4:30pm daily, closed Christmas Day
ADMISSION: $5 adults, $3.50 seniors and students, and children ages 13–17; $1.50 ages 5–12, children under 5 free
FURTHER INFORMATION FROM: 301 North Baldwin Avenue Arcadia 91007.
626.821.3222
NEARBY SIGHTS OF INTEREST: The Huntington, Descanso Gardens, Rancho Santa Ana Botanic Garden

29 Arcadia: The Arboretum of Los Angeles County

LOCATION: NORTH BALDWIN AVENUE, SOUTH OF FREEWAY 210 AND EAST OF HIGHWAY 19

Not far from downtown Los Angeles, tucked in close to the San Gabriel Mountains, is the Arboretum of Los Angeles County. Peacocks parade over its 127 acres, through 20 different garden areas that include a lake, a waterfall, and fountains. The arboretum is sited on the old Rancho Santa Anita, a 46,000-acre spread that had been owned by Elias Jackson "Lucky" Baldwin. Lucky Baldwin imported plants from all over the world, some of which—mostly trees such as ginkgoes, English oaks, eucalyptus, and Mexican fan palms—are found growing in the garden's historical section surrounding Baldwin's home. In 1885, Baldwin built the Queen Anne cottage and later a matching coach barn; both are listed on the National Register of Historic Places. Baldwin sold his home site to Harry Chandler in 1936, and the ranch was gradually whittled down by development. In 1947, Dr. Samuel Ayers came across the historic home site and persuaded Los Angeles County and the state to purchase 111 acres for an arboretum. The county later added 16 acres in two purchases, and was given the state's share of the title in 1989. Operated jointly by the county's Department of Parks and Recreation and the California Arboretum Foundation, the garden is arranged by geographical areas and theme gardens. You can stroll the grounds on paved pathways or view them via a tram that boards near the entrance. Contained within Circle Road is the historical section, with the home site, old-growth trees, and a rose garden. South of Circle Road is the Santa Anita Depot, built in 1890 by the Santa Fe Railroad using bricks from Baldwin's brickyard and reconstructed near the arboretum in 1970. To the west are garden areas for herbs and plants of the Southwest, South America, North America, and Asia. A waterfall and aquatic garden draw birds and other wildlife, and nearby in the meadowbrook area, 50 types of magnolias bloom in spring. North and east are sections devoted to plants of Africa and Australia. There are also theme gardens such as one featuring 200 colorful drought-tolerant landscape plants, and the Kallam Garden, featuring perennials, shrubs, and trees whose colors complement each other by season. Among the major plant collections are bottlebrush (*Callistemon*), acacias, cycads, red and orange-blooming coral trees, (*Erythrina*, the official tree of Los Angeles), eucalyptus, and paperbark trees (*Melaleuca*) with thick peeling bark. The arboretum's collection of 10,000 orchid species and hybrids, many of them

Baldwin Lake and Queen Anne Cottage at the Arboretum of Los Angeles County

housed in the tropical greenhouse, is among the nation's largest. As a horticultural and botanical center, the arboretum has introduced more than 100 flowering plants to the Southern California landscape.

GARDEN OPEN: 8am–5pm daily, closed New Year's Day, Independence Day, Thanksgiving, and Christmas Day

ADMISSION: Suggested donation of $2 adults, $5 families

FURTHER INFORMATION FROM: 1500 North College Avenue Claremont 91711-3101.
909.625.8767
www.rsabg.org

30 Claremont: Rancho Santa Ana Botanic Garden

LOCATION: ON COLLEGE AVENUE, OFF FOOTHILL BOULEVARD

In 1926, Susanna Bixby Bryant wrote to Dr. Charles Sprague Sargent, Arnold Professor of Aboriculture at Harvard University, outlining her vision for a botanical garden on her family's Santa Ana ranch in the foothills of the San Gabriel Mountains between Los Angeles and Riverside. Born at Rancho Los Alamitos, Bryant, a member of one of California's pioneering families, envisioned a garden that would represent California's native plants on her 200 acres. Sargent's response to the scheme was somewhat discouraging, but Bryant persisted, beginning work in the late 1920s with help from an accomplished horticulturist, a landscape architect, and a botanist. She built a fine adobe house, a library, and a herbarium, and began a native collection that grew significantly before her sudden death in 1946. Though the setting for Bryant's ambitious undertaking was spectacular, it was deemed too far removed from its research and teaching missions, and in 1950 the garden was moved to the Claremont College campus to be closer to the graduate program in botany. Fifty acres were laid out in a series of plant communities, and the first plantings of 10,000 trees and shrubs and 25,000 bulbs went in the next year. Today, the 86-acre site is the state's largest botanical garden dedicated exclusively to native California plants. With over 6,000 species, the state has the richest flora in the continental United States; this garden displays more than 2,800 California species, including 299 rare or endangered ones. The herbarium houses 975,000 specimens. The garden is laid out in three distinct areas. The Indian Hill Mesa, run-

Wildflower field at Rancho Santa Ana

ning north to south in the garden, is heavily planted with wild lilacs that bloom in spring in vivid shades of blue, violet, and white, and manzanitas with smooth red bark and intricate branching. Other gardens located on the mesa are an oak woodland, a southern riparian woodland, a basketry trail, a cultivar garden, and a home demonstration garden. The east alluvial gardens, include plants from the desert, the coast, and the Channel Islands, as well as an oasis containing California's only native palm, *Washingtonia filifera*. The 55 acres of plant communities, located in the northern part of the garden, display natives in their habitats, including madrone trees, piñon pines, flannel bushes, Catalina *Crossosoma*, the rare and endangered crucifixion thorn, and parry nolina, which project ten-foot rosettes with hundreds of cream-colored flowers in spring. The garden is a haven for birds (a checklist is available at the garden shop), and the local Audubon Society conducts bird walks from September through June on the first Sunday of the month.

GARDEN OPEN: 9am–5pm daily, closed Christmas Day
ADMISSION: $5 adult, $3 seniors and students, $1 children ages 5 to 11;
4 and under free; third Tuesday of the month free
FURTHER INFORMATION FROM:
26300 Crenshaw Boulevard
Palos Verdes Peninsula
90274.
310.544.6815

31 Palos Verdes Peninsula: South Coast Botanic Garden

LOCATION: SOUTH OF 405 FREEWAY AND WEST OF 110 FREEWAY

The innovative development of the South Coast Botanic Garden is one of the garden world's more unusual stories. This exciting experiment began in 1959, when the Los Angeles County Board of Supervisors, at the request of citizen and horticultural groups, agreed to create a botanic garden on three-and-a-half- million tons of garbage, on a site that in previous decades had been an open pit mine for diatomaceous earth. Overseen by the Los Angeles County Department of Arboreta and Botanic Gardens, the garden has become a classic example of land recycling and a model for horticulturists and administrators from around the world. In 1961, the first 40,000 plants—donated by individuals, nurseries, and the county arboretum, were planted on graded landfill. Since then, with assistance from the South Coast Botanic Garden Foundation, the garden has been developed over 87 acres of the Palos Verdes sanitary landfill. Gases formed underground as a result of decomposing refuse are collected throughout the landfill and are used to generate electricity. Five miles of paths, walkways, and roadways are left as undeveloped as possible to allow for ground settling. They connect some 20 distinct gardens arranged around a central lake and canal that attract ducks and heron (more than 200 bird species are sighted annually throughout the garden). Just east of the entrance are gardens managed by volunteers—including a screened area

with fuchsias, one devoted to cacti, others to bulbs and vegetables, and an "enchanted" children's garden with fairy tales interpreted through plants, topiary, figures, and architectural features. The All-American Rose Selections (AARS) garden features 1,600 top AARS roses from each year since 1945, including hybrids such as Double Delight and old-fashioned, fragrant roses. Raised beds filled with plants easily identified by touch, smell, and color groups invite visitors into the garden for the senses. Three color-scheme gardens—yellows with variegated leaves, blue flowers, and gray foliage—grace the south end of the garden. In the larger stretches of the north and west sides are tree collections, including pines, ginkgos, eucalyptus, ficus, palms, and pittosporum. Shaded by many of these mature trees, the trails are colorful year-round, with flowering plum and quince, coral trees, crape myrtle, sweet gum, and bottle brush. And if you'd rather ride than stroll the extensive grounds, a narrated tram tour is conducted three times a day on weekends.

32 Long Beach: Rancho Los Alamitos

LOCATION: PALO VERDE EXIT FROM THE **405** FREEWAY, HEAD SOUTH, THEN ENTER THROUGH THE BIXBY HILLS COMMUNITY

GARDEN OPEN: 1–5pm Wednesday–Sunday
ADMISSION: Free
FURTHER INFORMATION FROM:
6400 Bixby Hill Road
Long Beach, CA 90815.
562.431.3541

Stepping into the gardens at Rancho Los Alamitos is like stepping back into the early decades of the twentieth century, when ranch life was realized on a grand and gracious scale. Not that the gardens themselves are grandiose—far from it, they are beautifully designed, unpretentious, personal places that express the sensibilities of Florence Bixby. The wind-swept mesa had drawn people since 500 A.D., when it was part of the Native American Puvungna settlement area. In 1790, it was included in a 300,000-acre Spanish land grant awarded to soldier Manuel Nieto. By the time Fred and Florence Bixby moved in, the rancho land was reduced to around 7,000 acres of the 27,000 that Fred's parents John and Susan Bixby had purchased in 1881. Florence and Fred planted Canary Island date palms along a new driveway and transformed the property into a working horse ranch and headquarters for the Bixby ranches. Over the next 30 years, Florence Bixby extended the gardens

ABOVE: *Part of the ficus collection at South Coast Botanic Garden*

85

that Susan Bixby had begun, and designed a series of new gardens around the adobe ranch house with the help of renowned landscape architects Florence Yoch and Paul Howard. These were intimate spaces—a series of distinct outdoor "rooms" devoted to native plants, herbs, cacti, a "friendly" garden of plants given by friends, a tennis court and grape arbor, and a small walled secret garden. Those closer to the house were used as shaded private sitting areas and for entertaining, while the outer gardens were places for special plant collections. Through simple embellishments such as fountains, statues, and plaques, Florence Bixby revealed her interest in Mexican culture, Catholicism (a lovely Della Robbia Madonna, perhaps purchased on a trip to Italy, graces a gazebo wall), and traditions of rancho hospitality. Increasingly, the gardens and ranch house, flanked by two huge Moreton Bay figs, became an island of tranquility within a sea of change. Situated high on the hill overlooking their ranchland and the Pacific, the Bixbys could survey the encroaching development of Southern California. By

TOP: *A Moreton Bay fig*
BOTTOM: *The restored Geranium Walk*

the early 1930s, Florence created the outer gardens—the Oleander Walk, a rose garden, olive and cypress patios, and a cutting garden—to screen out urban sprawl prompted by the proliferation of oil wells that blocked their vistas to the south. These gardens and others were designed by the respected Olmsted Brothers landscape architecture firm, a fact that came to light only during recent historical research related to renovating the gardens. (Because of their historic and cultural significance, the south gardens have been restored with help from the state Office of Historic Preservation; restoration of the native garden is underway.) After Florence Bixby's death the family donated the inner seven-and-a-half acres around the house and gardens to the City of Long Beach in 1968. The site is operated by the Rancho Los Alamitos Foundation, which provides extensive educational programs on its cultural history. A visit to this beautifully detailed and elegant yet relaxed landscape provides a glimpse of Florence Bixby's generous spirit, which lives on in her gardens.

33 Fullerton: The Fullerton Arboretum

LOCATION: ON THE NORTHEAST CORNER OF THE CALIFORNIA STATE UNIVERSITY, FULLERTON CAMPUS, AT 1900 FULLERTON ROAD

In the late 1960s, when the northeast corner of the campus of the California State University, Fullerton was targeted to become a parking lot, a group of students and teachers insisted on green spaces and started organic gardening plots. Realizing the historical significance of the site's old orange grove, they proposed the creation of an arboretum. Opened in 1979, the now 26-acre Fullerton Arboretum officially was created in 1976 in an agreement between the university and the City of Fullerton. It is maintained and managed by the Fullerton Arboretum Authority, with help from the Friends of the Fullerton Arboretum. The garden's purpose is to provide a place for environmental, horticultural, and historical education, and to encourage research and experimentation in horticulture, plant ecology, and conservation of natural resources. It is also a quiet, esthetic retreat in the midst of urban development. A self-guided tour brochure, available free near the

GARDEN OPEN: 8am–4:45 pm, closed major holidays and special events
ADMISSION: Free (donations appreciated)
FURTHER INFORMATION FROM:
Fullerton Arboretum
c/o California State
University, Fullerton
P.O. Box 6850
Fullerton 92834-6850.
714.278.3579
www.arboretum.fullerton.edu
NEARBY SIGHTS OF INTEREST:
Rancho Los Alamitos,
Disneyland

Heritage House and pond

entrance, takes visitors through botanical collections that contain 3,000 plant species. The temperate zone features a conifer collection, carnivorous plant bog with insect-eating pitcher plants, a redwood grove, and primitive plants such as cycads. In the tropical zone around a large pond, the brilliant flowers of the bloody hand tree (*Chiranthodendron pentadactylon*) and coral trees mix with equally intriguing banyan and bo trees, a palm grove, and flowering tropical plants such as fragrant ginger lilies. The arid zone features native California plants such as white sage, monkeyflower, and island bush poppy, with collections of succulents, desert plants, and drought-tolerant plants from the Mediterranean region and South Africa, Chile, and Australia that adapt well to the dry Southern California environment. In the arboretum's center are cultivated collections of rare fruits, herbs, a children's garden and community and organic gardens, as well as a few remnant Valencia orange trees. "Old roses" are planted over four beds and climb a gazebo. The historical section of the arboretum reflects Orange County life around 1880-1910. The Heritage House, an Eastlake Victorian cottage built in 1894 as the home and office of a local physician and moved here in 1972, is open for docent-led tours from 2pm–4pm on Sundays. The house is surrounded by an orchard, a wisteria arbor, and gardens with annual and perennial flowers of the era.

GARDEN OPEN: 9am–4:30pm
Monday–Saturday,
10am–4pm Sunday
ADMISSION: $2.50
FURTHER INFORMATION FROM:
1701 South Palm Canyon
Drive
Palm Springs 92264.
760.327.6555

34 Palm Springs: Moorten Botanical
Garden

LOCATION: 1701 SOUTH PALM CANYON DRIVE

Patricia Moorten began her fantastical botanical garden in 1938 and moved it to its present site in Palm Springs in 1955, with the help of her late husband Chester "Cactus Slim" Moorten. Patricia was a research botanist who studied horticulture at the University of Southern California and the University of California, Los Angeles. It had been her dream since childhood to have a desert garden. "Desert plants are the highest forms of plant life," she says, because of their ability to live without water. One of her favorite types of desert plants was the ocotillo. Here on her ranch, she kept adding to her collection and cultivated cacti for botanical gardens around the world. Author of *Desert Plants for Desert Gardens*, she delighted in researching and displaying rare and unusual cacti, and in the 1940s built the first cactarium, a special greenhouse built into the ground for coolness. Today, the cactarium houses such rarities as Welwitschia, an odd-looking and difficult to grow African desert plant that

OPPOSITE: *Moorten
Botanical Garden in bloom*

produces only two leaves in its lifetime, and numerous showy euphorbias from Africa. In addition to the cactarium, over 3,000 varieties of desert plants are arranged over two-and-a-half acres in various dryland sections representing the Sonoran, Mojave, Californian, Mexican, African, and South American deserts. These include giant saguaro, organ pipe, prickly pear, and barrel cacti, yuccas, agaves, an octotillo forest, and ironwood trees, known for their exceptionally hard wood. Many of the plants are available for sale in the garden's nursery. Old West and Native American artifacts, pioneer relics, and props from film sets decorate the garden, delighting children especially. The Moorten ranch house, a Spanish-style, earthquake-proof, concrete and steel structure with two-foot-thick walls, originally built for artist Stephen Willard in 1929, adds a sense of southern California desert charm.

35 Palm Springs: The Living Desert

LOCATION: IN PALM DESERT, 15 MILES EAST OF PALM SPRINGS

Located at the far eastern edge of southern California at the foot of 12,000-foot Mt. San Jacinto, The Living Desert introduces us to the plants and wildlife of its own region and of far-flung lands. Established in 1970 as a 360-acre, nonprofit education and conservation center, The Living Desert is a zoological and botanical park that focuses on interpreting and preserving the deserts of the world. Its 1,800 acres include a 200-acre wildlife and botanical garden, a 1,000-acre wilderness preserve in Palm Desert, and a 600-acre preserve 15 miles south in the Santa Rosa Mountains. The focus of the zoological and botanical park is on ten desert ecosystems in North America and Africa. It eventually will also interpret the deserts of South America and Australia. It was one of the first botanic gardens to introduce the concept of landscape immersion, or replicating a habitat by changing the landscape with the plants, rocks, and landforms of a particular region. The Living Desert is home to the birds and animals of the region as well (some 150 creature species are represented). In the North American section are gardens representing the Baja, Mojave, Sonoran, and Chihuahuan deserts, a palm oasis and walk-through aviary, a demonstration garden showcasing Southwestern plants in native landscapes,

GARDEN OPEN: 9am–5pm (last admission 4pm) daily September–June 15, 8am–1:30pm June 16–August 31, closed Christmas Day
ADMISSION: $8.50 adults, $7.50 seniors and military, $4.25 children ages 3-12, children under 3 free
FURTHER INFORMATION FROM: 47-900 Portola Avenue Palm Desert 92260. 760.346.5694 www.livingdesert.org
NEARBY SIGHTS OF INTEREST: Moorten Botanical Garden, Palm Springs Aerial Tramway, Palm Springs Desert Museum

and a Native American ethnobotanical garden focusing on the life of the local Cahuillas. Reflecting the local plant life, the Upper Colorado River Desert area is filled with native trees and plants—palo verdes, smokewoods, desert willows, verbenas, salvias, and beaver tail and cholla cacti. More than 125 varieties of desert plants, from agaves to scarlet bugler penstemon to Mexican blue sage, grow at The Living Desert and are sold in the garden center near the café and amphitheater. These are hardy, drought-tolerant species that can withstand temperatures ranging from below freezing to 120 degrees Fahrenheit (or 145 degrees on the sand). In the garden's Village WaTuTu, African animals such as camels, leopards, gazelles, and zebras range among acacias and thorn trees. A wilderness loop trail leads from the desert floor at 300 feet in elevation to the top of 1,952-foot Eisenhower Mountain.

The demonstration garden is part of a water conservation project to educate the public on how native plants can beautify home gardens. Shown are: agave, Mexican fan palms, and ocotillo.

36 Corona Del Mar: Sherman Library and Gardens

LOCATION: ON THE PACIFIC COAST HIGHWAY

Garden lovers and history buffs alike will appreciate the Sherman Library and Gardens, a distinctive educational and cultural center named for Moses H. Sherman (1853-1932)—educator, railway entrepreneur, and California pioneer. Encompassing a full city block along the Pacific Coast Highway, the library and gardens began modestly in 1966. The land was acquired and construction began under the leadership of local businessman Arnold D. Haskell, the principal founder and benefactor of the Sherman Foundation, and a longtime associate of Sherman's. The adobe and tiled-roof library is a historical research center devoted to the study of the Pacific Southwest, including California, Arizona, and portions of Nevada and the Baja region. Its resources—including 15,000 books and pamphlets, sizable collections of maps and photographs, more than 2,000 reels of microfilm (including old newspaper files), and 200,000 papers and documents—chronicle the remarkable transformation of the region over the past 100 years. Surrounding the library on more than two acres is a series of humanly scaled and meticulously tended garden rooms that represent plants from more far-flung regions. In a setting of blue-tiled fountains, sculpture, and manicured lawns, the botanical collections contain more than 1,000 species that range from dryland desert plants to tropical varieties. The gardens radiate from an octagonal central court with a reflecting pool. Surrounding a large California pepper tree are the cactus and succulents gardens. Other outdoor "rooms" include a fuchsia collection and a palm garden with 40 specimens, including king palms. Tiled walks, many with arbors, lead to a shade garden with tuberous begonias and a fern grotto festooned with staghorn ferns. Dozens of varieties of climbers, floribundas, and hybrid teas bloom in the rose garden, and the island-like discovery garden invites visitors to touch and smell plants such as scented geraniums, pineapple sage, lavender, and lamb's ear. Orchids, gingers, bromeliads, anthuriums, and bright heliconias from the Pacific Islands flourish in the humid tropical conservatory around a stone pool stocked with shimmering koi. Throughout the grounds, flower beds, large pots, and hanging baskets of annuals provide colorful and fragrant settings for weddings and other events. A café serves lunch and an outdoor tea garden presents high tea five days a week.

GARDEN OPEN: 10:30am–4pm daily, closed New Year's Day, Thanksgiving, and Christmas Day
LIBRARY OPEN: 9am–4pm, Tuesday –Thursday
ADMISSION: $3 adults, $1 children ages 12–16, under 12 free, Mondays free
FURTHER INFORMATION FROM: 2647 East Coast Highway Corona del Mar 92625. 949.673.2261

One of Sherman Library's many outdoor rooms, this one blooming with foxglove

GARDEN OPEN: By advance
reservation only
ADMISSION: Free, donations
appreciated
FURTHER INFORMATION FROM:
Friends of Hortense Miller
Garden
PO Box 742
Laguna Beach 92652.
949.497.0716 (Laguna Beach
Recreation Department)

37 Laguna Beach: Hortense Miller Garden

LOCATION: IN ALLVIEW TERRACE (PRIVATE COMMUNITY)

Hortense Miller began her garden at her new home on the upper slopes of Boat Canyon in 1959, at the age of 50. With the help of a gardener one day a week, she started planting the two-and-a-half acres, putting in paths, steps, and bamboo fencing. The native vegetation was sparse, save the sugar gum eucalyptus trees in front of the house. Year after year, she pulled a wilderness of foxtail grass. She planted what people gave her or small plants she had purchased. Now 92 and still active in her garden, she presides over a richly textured garden that includes 1,500 plant species from around the world. Some of the plants in the garden are laced with nostalgia, favorites from when she was a little girl in St. Louis—day lilies, sunflowers, black locust, rose acacia, tansy, and rose-mallow. Her tiger lily bed derived from a single bulb given to Miller when she was 15 years old. Because of the garden's mild climate—ocean breezes waft in from the Pacific half a mile away—a wide variety of plants from subtropical zones of the Americas, South Africa, Australia, and the Mediterranean thrive here. The house and garden provide walls and fences on which flourish wisteria, jasmine, and bougainvillea. The central part of the garden is divided into five distinct and intimate "rooms." The entrance court is draped with lilac-colored Japanese wisteria. The gazebo garden, poised on a hill of Korean grass and golden bamboo, graces the inner patio. Next to the ponds is a dry garden featuring a rare *Euphorbia* tree, eucalyptuses, and a slope covered with blooming iceplant. On the sunnier side of the house, old-fashioned favorites and newer hybrids mix in the perennial garden with bulbs such as amaryllis and americrinums. A pink, double-flowering cherry tree is a spectacular sight set against the blue sky and ocean in early spring. On the canyon side of the house, an Easter lily vine (*Beaumontia grandiflora*) overlooks a garden of Matilija poppies and iris. Further down the path is a seating area with a backdrop of passion vine. Salvias, succulents, aloes, and rare puyas from Chile bloom in the lower entrance area. Paths also lead to wild areas rife with native coastal sage scrub, California holly (*Toyon*), lemonade berry, and perennials such as bush lupines, penstemon, and blue-eyed grass. A devastating fire swept through the canyon and garden in 1979, destroying many native plants but also redistributing plant communities and causing the germination of many beautiful new hybrids. Hortense Miller saw this as part of Mother

Nature's plan for her garden, a rejuvenation that complemented her original plan. Miller has willed her home and garden to the City of Laguna Beach for use as a public park, and the city's recreation department schedules tours that are led by members of the Friends of the Hortense Miller Garden.

38 Encinitas: Quail Botanical Gardens

LOCATION: ON QUAIL GARDENS DRIVE

Framed in a photograph in the main house at the Quail Botanical Gardens is the lovely face of a young Ruth Baird Larabee, who founded the gardens over a half century ago. In 1943, when Ruth Larabee was 28, she and her husband Charles bought 26 acres of ranchland on the coast north of San Diego. The terrain was rugged and dry, with chaparral covering sunny hillsides, deep eroded canyons, and views of the Pacific Ocean. An avid plant collector, Ruth soon began planting exotic specimens she brought back from Mexico and Central and South America—unusual varieties like a Mexican handflower tree,

GARDEN OPEN: 9am–5pm daily, closed New Year's Day, Thanksgiving, and Christmas Day

ADMISSION: $5 adult, $4 seniors, $2 ages 5-12, children under 5 free, first Tuesday of month free

TOURS: 10am Saturday, free; children's tours 10:30am first Tuesday of month

FURTHER INFORMATION FROM: PO Box 5
230 Quail Gardens Drive
Encinitas 92024.
760.436.3036
www.qbgardens.com

A restful spot under palms at Quail Botanical Gardens

whose claw-like brown flowers were used by the Aztecs as medicine for heart problems. Inspired by the sandy soil and mild climate, she planted subtropical fruit-bearing plants and trees, cork oaks, palms, cycads, aloes, cacti, and hibiscus. Dressed in dungarees and rubber boots, she would haul buckets of water from Cottonwood Creek to keep the plants alive. She had adobe walls built to enclose the garden around her 1917 house. Dubbed El Rancho de las Flores, the property was transformed by her vision to create a natural place for the public's enjoyment and children's education. In 1957, however, her life changed dramatically. She divorced from Charles and planned to nurse the poor in Mexico, and deeded her home and garden to San Diego County, provided that a few acres be put aside for the native quail that roam the area. Three years later, the Quail Botanical Gardens Foundation was formed to preserve and support her creation. Over the next 30 years, the county and foundation created a master plan for a botanical garden, installed irrigation, public facilities, and a 150-foot waterfall, and opened the gardens to the public. Quail became a private nonprofit organization operated by the foundation in 1993, and since then has been expanded to represent flora from around the world. Arranged geographically according to climates, the gardens range from desert plants of the Baja region and Madagascar to subtropical plants from the Himalayas and the Pacific Islands, to plants of the Mediterranean climates. One demonstration garden contains the continent's largest collection of bamboos, another an exhibit of native plants and people, focusing on a Kumeyaay Indian homesite and native plant trail. Garden activities often are hosted at the Ecke Building, donated in 1971 with four additional acres by Paul and Magdalena Ecke.

39 San Diego: Balboa Park

LOCATION: JUST NORTH OF DOWNTOWN SAN DIEGO, BETWEEN HIGHWAY 163 AND PARK BOULEVARD

Balboa Park's history is as colorful as the 1,200-acre park is diverse. It is home to the San Diego Zoo, 15 museums, and numerous performing arts groups, as well as many cultural and recreational groups. First established in 1868 as the 1,400-acre City Park, it consisted mostly of barren mesa tops and canyons. It is now one of the nation's lushest urban parks, thanks to horticulturist Kate O. Sessions ("the mother of Balboa Park"), who in the late 1800s and early 1900s planted hundreds of trees every year in exchange for land to develop her own 30-acre horticultural nursery. More than 15,000 trees of some 350 species now provide shade and beauty throughout the park. The park's landmark tree is a Moreton Bay fig, and

other notable trees are a Brazilian parrot's beak with bright red blooms and towering Canary Island pines and Australian sugar gums. Sessions also planted the original Mexican fan palms in the palm canyon, which features 450 palm trees of 58 species (self-guided tour maps of Session's plantings and specific gardens are available at the visitor information center in the House of Hospitality). Renamed Balboa Park in 1910 in honor of the Spanish explorer, the park was developed further with many new Spanish colonial-style buildings and landscape plantings for the 1915 Panama-California Exposition. The botanical building, the world's largest wood lath structure when it was built for the exposition, contains a permanent collection of 2,100 tropical plants with changing seasonal flowers. The lily pond just south of it is an eloquent example of the use of reflecting pools to enhance architecture. Eight distinct garden areas are arranged amidst these and other historic buildings constructed for the 1935 California-Pacific International Exposition. Adjacent to the House of Charm, the Alcazar Garden—reconstructed to replicate a 1935 design by San Diego architect Richard Requa—recalls the gardens of Alcazar Castle in Seville, Spain, with ornate fountains, exquisite turquoise, yellow, and green Moorish tiles, boxwood hedges, and thousands of brilliant annual flowers. The old cactus garden, also developed for the 1935 exposition, contains large cacti and succulents and exotic African and Australian proteas. A formal English romantic-style garden graces the Marston House at 3525 Seventh Avenue, where many of the mature trees were planted by Kate Sessions in 1906. The grounds were designed by renowned landscape architects George Cook, John Nolen, Thomas Church, and Hal Walker. Walker and William Templeton Johnson designed the formal garden in 1927 to honor George White's and Anna Gunn Marston's 50th anniversary. A desert garden near the Natural History Museum encompasses two-and-a-half acres with 1,300 drought-resistant plants whose peak blooming period is January through March. From March through December, the Inez Grant Parker Memorial Rose Garden is flush with colors and fragrances of some 2,400 rose bushes. This award-winning All American Rose Selections display garden features 180 varieties. The strolling paths, koi pond, and wisteria arbor of the Japanese Friendship Garden suggest places for quiet reflection, while in the Zoro Garden, butterflies flit from lantana to verbena within the sunken stone grotto. In the California native plant demonstration garden, located near Balboa Park's tennis courts, a loop trail displays three dozen native species, such as tall coast sunflow-

GARDEN OPEN: Dawn to dusk daily

ADMISSION: Free (fee for zoo and Japanese Friendship Garden)

TOURS: Free plant and history walks 10am every Saturday from January through November

FURTHER INFORMATION FROM:
Park & Recreation Department
City of San Diego
Balboa Park Management Center
San Diego 92101.
619.239.0512
(for information about tours and free tram service to parking, call 619.235.1121; for zoo information call 619.234.3153)

NEARBY SITES OF INTEREST:
San Diego Zoo, Museum of Art, Natural History Museum, all within the park

Inez Grant Parker Memorial Rose Garden

ers and sagebrush, western redbud tree with showy magenta flowers, and Baja Bush-snapdragon, a small evergreen shrub whose red tubular flowers attract hummingbirds. The world-class San Diego Zoo botanical collection, with 6,000 plant species, includes prized orchids, cycads, fig trees, palms, and coral trees.

Zoro Butterfly Garden

40 Reno: Wilbur D. May Arboretum & Botanical Garden

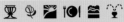

LOCATION: WITHIN RANCHO SAN RAFAEL PARK, NORTH OF INTERSTATE 80

The 12-acre Wilbur D. May Arboretum and Botanical Garden is a living museum, the main purpose of which is to research and demonstrate the botanical possibilities in the high desert environment. Located in a transitional zone between the Sierra Nevada Mountains and the Great Basin Desert, the garden receives only seven inches of precipitation a year and has a growing season of less than 100 days. At 4,600 feet, the garden's daily temperature can vary 50 degrees or more. Numerous gardens and groves, including a xeriscape demonstration garden, feature the regional trees and shrubs, such as piñon pine, juniper, and salt desert shrub, and wildflowers such as giant evening primrose, Mexican hat, and lance-leaved coreopsis. Pathways connect these gardens and groves to a series of ornamental gardens, including rock, cactus, butterfly, and rose gardens. Flowering perennials bloom in the Burke Garden, designed in the English country style, and yellow and white-flowering roses and shrubs rim a cascade and pools in Honey's Garden. The Songbird Garden features food, water, and shelter with more than 200 species of shrubs and trees that attract goldfinches, western meadowlarks, warblers, and hummingbirds. The indoor arboretum is a tropical retreat featuring a waterfall, ponds stocked with koi, and plants such as palms. The arboretum and botanical garden are part of the Wilbur D. May Center, which was created by a foundation honoring local philanthropist Wilbur D. May, the son of David May, founder of the May Department Stores. A collector, businessman, rancher, composer, artist, pilot, and big game hunter, May lived in Reno from 1936 until his death in 1982. The grounds also include a museum of artifacts (including rare T'ang Dynasty pottery) that May amassed during some 40 trips around the world, and Great Basin Adventure, designed for children with attractions such as a petting zoo and a wetland-habitat nature walk. The center is located within the 600-acre Rancho San Rafael Park, which is owned and managed by the Washoe County Parks and Recreation Department.

GARDEN OPEN: 10am–5pm, Tuesday–Sunday in summer, Wednesday–Sunday in winter

TOURS: Available upon request. Self-guided trail map also available.

ADMISSION: Free

FURTHER INFORMATION FROM:
1502 Washington Street
Reno 89503.
775.785.4153

NEARBY SIGHTS OF INTEREST:
Wilbur D. May Museum and Great Basin Adventure, both within Rancho San Rafael Park, and University of Nevada, Reno

Creamy yucca flowers bloom in the desert.

GARDEN OPEN: 8:30am–7pm
daily; closed Christmas Day
ADMISSION: Free
TOURS: Free guided tours
offered for 10 or more guests
FURTHER INFORMATION FROM:
2 Cactus Garden Drive
Henderson 89014.
702.458.8864 or
1.888.627.0990

41 Henderson: Ethel M. Chocolate Factory Botanical Garden

LOCATION: OFF HIGHWAY 93, ON SUNSET ROAD EAST OF MOUNTAIN VISTA

When Forrest Mars, Sr. retired to Las Vegas, having managed the family confections business that his parents, Frank and Ethel Mars, had started in 1911 in their Tacoma, Washington kitchen, he wanted to return to his roots: chocolate. So in 1981, he opened the Ethel M. Chocolate Factory, located just outside of Las Vegas. At his new factory, he wanted a landscape that would provide pleasure for his employees. Having visited The Huntington botanical gardens in San Marino, California, he asked for their assistance in creating a glorious desert garden. Gary Lyons, a designer for The Huntington, came to Las Vegas and created a plan for the garden, using naturalistic landscape design ideas that respected the region's need to conserve water. Over the past two decades, the original one-acre garden has expanded to four acres of drought-tolerant ornamentals, cacti, and other succulents. With a landscape base of 15,000 cubic yards of sandy fill and a special planting soil, the beds were raised and rockeries constructed with 400 tons of Utah Bali Hai "chocolate" rock and Arizona moss rock from the Grand Canyon region. The garden displays more than 300 species of plants. Half are cacti and succulents native to the Southwest, and the rest are desert trees and shrubs from the Southwest, Australia, and South America chosen for their aesthetic qualities and their ability to adapt to southern Nevada. What little water the gardens do require is supplied by using the factory's gray water for irrigation. Highlights of the cactus collection include clumping hedgehogs, producing pink and violet blossoms in spring, and fish hook barrels, whose more delicate orange flowers bloom in August and September. In the Australian display, an odd but graceful shoestring acaria has an open-branched, weeping posture that earns the nickname "the tree that gives no shade." Near the Australian section, the attractive but notorious yellow-spined teddy bear cholla is planted at a safe distance from curious little bodies. Some of the largest displays are of Nevada cacti from the Mojave Desert and the province of Sonora. Key among them are ocotillo, prickly pear, compass barrel, and pygmy barrel, all of which grow in the foothills of the Las Vegas Valley. Interesting shrubs such as red- and yellow-flowering desert bird of paradise and desert willow mix with native and exotic wildflowers such as Australia's Sturt's desert pea, which keeps its low feathery foliage and large deep-red flowers until September. The garden has something in bloom most seasons. From early December through early January, it blazes with 200,000 lights draped through the cacti.

OPPOSITE: Ocotillo and towering cacti at the Ethel M.Chocolate factory and Botanical Garden

25
SPOKANE

SEATTLE 17-23

16 26,27

31 TACOMA 29,30

24

28

WASHINGTON

PORTLAND
1-7

8   9

SALEM 10,11

EUGENE 12-14

15
COOS BAY

OREGON

NORTHWEST

Oregon, Washington

With temperate summers and plenty of rain year-round, it's not surprising that the native landscape of the Pacific Northwest offers multiple sublime shades of green. Early garden makers in the region found the mild, rainy climate encouraged most plants to grow bigger, better, and faster. Financed by the railroads, the timber industry, and the Alaska Gold Rush, the Pacific Northwest barons began creating elaborate estate gardens in the first decade of the twentieth century, many of them rivaling what East Coast gardens developed over the course of 300 years. The Alaska-Yukon-Pacific Exposition of 1909 in Seattle influenced Northwest gardens by piquing interest in all things Asian, especially aspects of Chinese and Japanese culture. Many of the region's gardens of the early and mid-century looked to the East in their designs and plant materials.

Though a city plan for Tacoma by renowned landscape architect Frederick Law Olmsted was rejected in 1874 as too curvilinear, the Olmsted Brothers firm of Brookline, Massachusetts, soon helped transform the region. The Olmsteds' particular style of naturalistic, richly layered and textured gardens appealed to Northwesterners and complemented the beauty of their native plants. Lured to Seattle to plan the 1905 Lewis and Clark Exposition, the firm over the next 30 years also designed nearly 60 private gardens in Portland, Seattle, and Spokane. The Olmsteds also induced Emil T. Mische to come to Portland, where he designed the city's park system and was its superintendent during the formative years between 1908 and

OPPOSITE: *View of the Japanese maple collection at the Bloedel Reserve*

1914. Other respected landscape designers trained on the East Coast included Elizabeth Lord and Edith Schryver, who formed the region's first woman-run landscape architecture firm. Toward the middle of the century, other gifted landscape architects from the West Coast, including Thomas Church, influenced Northwest gardens by introducing a modern, artistic, often sculptural style of garden design.

In Washington, the Olmsteds designed parks in Spokane and Seattle, as well as private gardens such as the Dunn Estate. Near Tacoma, Lakewold Gardens were laid out originally by the Olmsted firm, and later reshaped and replanted under the direction of Church and accomplished plant collector Eulalie Wagner, who owned the estate with her husband Corydon. Her sister, Virginia Merrill Bloedel, and her husband Prentice, with Church and other designers created one of the country's finest estate landscapes, the Bloedel Reserve on Bainbridge Island. Other public gardens created since the mid-century, such as the Carl S. English, Jr. Gardens in Seattle, the Ohme Gardens in Wenatchee, and the Chase Garden in Orting, display the passions of their individual creators.

In Oregon, the first three decades of the twentieth century were equally prolific. In 1905, the Olmsteds designed Elk Rock in Portland, an elegant series of terraced gardens with a lawn and richly layered border of native shrubs and trees—madrones, Douglas firs, cedars, western dogwood, Oregon grape—woven into the design. The use of natives in gardens was new for the region, and set the tone for a style of garden design that continues today. Elk Rock also established a garden tradition of using a sophisticated horticultural mix of natives with exotic specimen plants favored by the estate's builder, grain merchant and plant collector Peter Kerr. West and south of Portland, the Jenkins Estate and Shore Acres

State Park, originally a garden estate built by lumber baron Louis J. Simpson, also took shape during the early years of the century. Two Portland-area gardens, now known as the Berry Botanic Garden and the Leach Botanical Garden, were established in the 1920s and 30s by two accomplished plantswomen, Rae Selling Berry, who specialized in rare rhododendrons from China and Tibet, and Lilla Leach, an explorer and grower of ornamental native species. Laid out in 1917 on terraces high above Portland, the International Rose Test Garden at Washington Park, the oldest rose test garden in the country, began Portland's tradition as the "City of Roses." In Salem, Lord and Schryver designed exquisite garden rooms for the Deepwood Estate and for Bush's Pasture Park, which offers the region's finest collection of old roses.

View across Middle Pond toward Visitor Center at the Bloedel Reserve. Weeping willow on left; tundra swan on pond

GARDEN OPEN: 7am–9pm daily

ADMISSION: Free (donations welcome)

FURTHER INFORMATION FROM:
Portland Public Rose Gardens
400 SW Kingston Avenue
Portland 97205.
503.823.3636

NEARBY SIGHTS OF INTEREST:
The Japanese Garden in Washington Park, Hoyt Arboretum

I

Portland: International Rose Test Garden

LOCATION: IN PORTLAND'S WASHINGTON PARK, ACROSS FROM THE JAPANESE GARDEN

Portland is known as the "City of Roses," and nowhere in this region is there a more lavish show than in Washington Park's International Rose Test Garden. From the grand stone entrance stairway, the garden unfurls on terraces below like a great patchwork quilt made of vivid rose chintzes in hues ranging from crisp whites to romantic mauves to rich reds and golds. The garden spans four-and-a-half acres with 8,000 roses of some 560 labeled varieties. During World War I, leading American nurserymen were searching for a site to replace European test gardens that had been closed. Jesse A. Currey, the garden's first curator, was instrumental in establishing the test garden in Portland. Founded in 1917, it is the oldest continuously operated public rose test garden in the United States. In the years following, it grew larger and its bones more elaborate. During the Great Depression, the Works Progress Administration constructed the extensive and detailed stonework stairways and terraces with basalt from central Oregon. The All-American Rose Selections Garden on the upper terrace is the largest and perhaps the most impressive section of the garden, particularly because of its panoramic views of Portland and Mount Hood. Here you'll find beds with plants identified by code numbers rather than names. Four plants for each entry are scored on 15 different points for two years. These beds also display the American Rose Society's miniature test roses. The formal Royal Rosarian Garden honors the service organization's key members with namesake roses. At the south end is the Gold Medal Garden, where a gazebo offers a place to enjoy the award-winning blooms planted in beds radiating from a central brick fountain. On the terrace below, in the southeast corner, is the Shakespeare Garden.

Artistry Coral Rose from the International Rose Test Garden

Screened by large yews, it is a quiet place to savor fragrant borders filled with roses, herbs, and flowers mentioned in the Bard's work. Back on the upper terrace, a modern stainless-steel sculptural fountain dedicated to Frank E. Beach, who gave Portland its nickname, provides cooling water music for hot summer days in the garden.

2 Portland: The Japanese Garden in Washington Park

LOCATION: 611 SW KINGSTON AVENUE, WITHIN WASHINGTON PARK

When you enter the traditional tile-roofed gate at the Japanese Garden in Washington Park, be prepared to leave the bustling world behind. Although a very popular place, the garden exerts an overwhelming sense of peace, harmony, and tranquility. Considered one of the most authentic Japanese gardens outside of Japan, this landscape emphasizes plants, stones, and water—the essence of nature, influenced by ancient Shinto, Buddhist, and Taoist philosophies. This private, nonprofit garden was founded in 1962 and opened to the public in 1967 by a group of Portland citizens that formed the Japanese Garden Society of Oregon. Professor Takuma Tono, an internationally renowned authority on Japanese landscapes, designed the garden. It encompasses five-and-a-half acres and five distinct garden styles: the strolling pond garden, the tea garden, the natural garden, the dry garden, and the flat garden. The largest is the strolling pond garden, which you enter through a wisteria arbor. A moon bridge crosses the upper pond. A zig-zag bridge traverses dark waters where koi glide silently past beds of purple and white iris. To the south is the lower pond with tortoise and crane stones that symbolize longevity. A 20-foot waterfall splashes into the pond, which is encircled by Japanese maples, rhododendrons, and azaleas. Other waterfalls and shallow streams meander downhill through the nat-

GARDEN OPEN: 10am–7pm daily April 1–September 30. 10am–4pm daily in winter
ADMISSION: $6, $4 seniors, $3.50 students; children 5 and under free
FURTHER INFORMATION FROM: The Japanese Garden Society of Oregon
P.O. Box 3847
Portland 97208-3847.
503.223.4070
www.japanesegarden.com

Raked sand in the flat garden suggests rings of water in a pond

ural garden. The path through this garden is a contrast of rough chunks of stone and smooth granite slabs reused from an old civic stadium in Portland—an example of the Japanese garden principle of recycling materials and incorporating the surrounding environment. The dry landscape, the most abstract of Japanese garden forms, is typical of the contemplative gardens of Buddhist monasteries in Japan. Within this simple, walled garden is a stone bed raked into waves that lap at jagged, weathered rocks. Dappled sunlight filters through the overstory, creating a subtle and calming sense of movement on the stones. The path leading to the south side of the pavilion passes by a fountain of stone and bamboo. From the pavilion's east deck there is a spectacular view of Portland and Mount Hood. The deck on the west side embraces an intimate view of the flat garden. A lovely pink weeping cherry graces the "pond" of pale gray sand, which is raked to suggest the rings created by a stone in still water. Ripples of raked sand follows the contours of small islands that depict a sake cup and gourd bottle, signifying pleasure and a wish for the visitor's happiness.

GARDEN OPEN: Dawn to dusk daily. Visitor center open from 9am–3pm

TOURS: Saturdays and Sundays from April through October

ADMISSION: Free

FURTHER INFORMATION FROM: 4000 SW Fairview Boulevard Portland 97221.
503.228.8733

NEARBY SIGHTS OF INTEREST: International Rose Test Garden and Japanese Garden (both in Washington Park)

3 Portland: Hoyt Arboretum

LOCATION: ON FAIRVIEW BOULEVARD, NEAR WASHINGTON PARK AND ZOO

Hoyt Arboretum's ten miles of scenic hiking trails wind through Portland's western hills, offering cityscape and mountain views and connecting to the city's 40-mile loop trail system. But even if you're not interested in trekking that distance, you can still enjoy many of the arboretum's 800 species of labeled trees and shrubs. Established in 1928 and owned by the city, the collection includes 100-year old native trees, as well as plants from six continents, such as Chilean monkey puzzle trees, fragrant Asian magnolias, European weeping beech, cedars from North Africa, and Oregon's own rarity, the Brewer's weeping spruce. Conifers include Himalayan spruce, dawn redwood, Chinese lacebark pine, and a grove of coast and giant redwoods. The bristlecone pine trail and the Oregon Vietnam Veterans Memorial Trail are wheelchair accessible. The wildflower walk begins just across the street from the visitor center and follows a one-and-three-quarter-mile loop. Along the path are dozens of varieties of wildflowers, such as spring-blooming trilliums, star flowers, columbine, wild ginger, and the whimsically monikered duck's foot inside-out flower (*Vancouveria hexandra*). Summer brings Columbia lilies, fireweed, self-heal, and wild sweet peas. A wildflower walk map and various other maps and brochures are available at the visitor center; while there, check out the hardiness test garden of mixed perennials.

4 Portland: The Berry Botanic Garden

LOCATION: SW SUMMERVILLE AVENUE, OFF MILITARY ROAD, BETWEEN LAKE
OSWEGO AND PORTLAND

GARDEN OPEN: Daylight
hours, by appointment
ADMISSION: $5 for adults 18
and over
FURTHER INFORMATION FROM:
11505 S.W. Summerville
Avenue
Portland 97219.
503.636.4112
NEARBY SIGHTS OF INTEREST:
Elk Rock Garden at Bishop's
Close

Nestled in the rolling hills southwest of Portland, the Berry
Botanic Garden invites visitors to experience the gentle, naturalistic garden style of a celebrated plantswoman, Rae Selling
Berry. An avid gardener, Berry supported British plant expeditions in the early 1900s, planting seeds collected in the
wilds of Asia and Europe in her own northeast Portland garden. In 1938, when she ran out of space for her exotic collection, she and her husband, Alfred Berry, an Englishman
raised in India, selected the garden's current bowl-shaped
site on a ridge just north of Lake Oswego, near the
Willamette River. The six-acre site of their new home
spanned different microclimates for her collection—springs,
creeks, a ravine, a meadow, and slopes covered with second-
growth Douglas fir. Well-known Seattle landscape architect
John Grant designed the tree placements and the lawn, now
bordered with primroses, tree peonies, and giant Himalayan
lilies. Berry designed and planted most of the garden according to the needs of her plants, including many alpines and
primroses that she collected on treks throughout the Pacific
Northwest, British Columbia, and Alaska. She was particularly fond of the only native primrose in Oregon, *Primula
cusickiana*, which she called her "problem child," and dubbed
"Cooky." She cultivated many rare rhododendrons from
China and Tibet; at the age of 90, she was planting rhododendron seed destined to mature years later. The garden's
species rhododendron forest contains 150 different plants,
some 20 feet tall and a half-century old. After Berry's death
in 1976, a nonprofit friends group continued her legacy.
Today, her historical garden is honored, though the plants
increasingly reflect a mission of displaying Northwest natives
that are appropriate for home gardens. The expansive rock
garden west and south of the house features native spireas,
sun roses, and golden drops. Around the gazebo are tall
native meadowrues, penstemons, and filberts with fountain-
like trunks. The nearby greenhouse displays native monkey
flowers and pink checker mallows. An unusual and delightful
area west of the house displays numerous trough gardens,
inspired by the English gardening tradition popular in the
1920s and 30s. Ranging in size and shape, the synthetic concrete troughs brim with tiny native heathers, ferns, sax-
ifrages, sedums, and mosses. In this elegant home garden of
many layers, Berry's love of exotic plants is combined with
interesting native species to create a subtle and complex experience for horticulturists.

GARDEN OPEN: 8am–5pm
daily, except holidays

ADMISSION: Free

FURTHER INFORMATION FROM:
11800 SW Military Lane
Portland 97219.
503.636.5613

NEARBY SIGHTS OF INTEREST:
The Berry Botanic Garden

5 Portland: Elk Rock Garden at Bishop's Close

LOCATION: SW MILITARY LANE, OFF ROUTE 43, BETWEEN LAKE OSWEGO AND
PORTLAND

On a bluff over the Willamette River with a view of Mount
Hood, Elk Rock, the garden of the Bishop's Close, is a quiet,
contemplative place that offers a glimpse of the pre-World
War I estate-garden world of elegant design and horticultural
mastery. Off the beaten path in an exclusive residential area,
the Elk Rock garden seems even more removed from the con-
temporary world with its grassy expanses, far-off vistas, and
intimate gardens of the senses. In the early 1890s, a wealthy
local grain merchant, a Scotsman named Peter Kerr, bought
the 13-acre parcel with his brother Thomas and partner Patrick
Gifford. The three bachelors lived in a cottage on the edge of
the cliff. In 1910, Kerr hired John Olmsted of the renowned
Olmsted Brothers to site a larger house and help design the
layout for the grounds around it. When the Scottish manor
house, designed by D.E Lawrence, was finished in 1916, Kerr,
an ardent gardener and plant collector, began creating one of
the great gardens of the Northwest. His efforts transformed
the site into a pastoral landscape with a great lawn and many-
layered, naturalistic borders of both exotic and native shrubs
and trees, with smaller flower gardens close by the house.
Kerr renamed his estate Elk Rock after a legend that the local
Indians hunted elk by running them off the cliff. In 1957,
when Kerr died at the age of 95, his daughters, Anne

*A naturalistic, John
Olmstead-designed path with
fountain*

McDonald and Jane Platt, gave Elk Rock to the Episcopal Bishop of Oregon with an endowment for the care and maintenance of the garden, provided it was open to the public. Since 1986, a garden committee has managed the landscape. A brochure with a self-guided tour is available at the visitor's center on the west side of the house, near a low, cobalt-blue fountain designed by Lee Kelly. On the east side of the house, just outside the chapel, is a small walled garden with fragrant herbs such as lavender and santolina. Beyond it is a grove bordering the great lawn with magnolias, a golden rain tree, giant sequoia, and a dove tree. Shrubs such as wintersweet, the Oregon native silk tassel, and a large and rare *Stachyurus praecox* provide layers of color and texture beneath them. The Spring Walk is famous for its winter-blooming viburnums and buttercup winter hazel beneath trees including a rare Katsura and a dawn redwood. Just before a bridge, the cascades area features trees with interesting barks, such as birches and paper-barked maple. On the south lawn, an Atlas cedar towers above numerous magnolias, and paths to a viewpoint and the upper south lawn mix native and exotic trees, including Japanese cornelian cherry, Alaskan yellow cedar, and madrones. An upper trail leads through an allée of yews to a semi-circular boxwood parterre displaying a spectacular collection of witch hazels.

6   Portland: Crystal Springs Rhododendron Garden

LOCATION: SE 28TH AVENUE, ONE BLOCK NORTH OF WOODSTOCK, BETWEEN
REED COLLEGE AND EASTMORELAND GOLF COURSE

GARDEN OPEN: Dawn to dusk daily

ADMISSION: $3 from March 1–Labor Day (10am–6pm); free on Tuesday and Wednesday and for children under 12

FURTHER INFORMATION FROM:
SE 28th and Woodstock
Portland 97202.
503.771.8386
www.parks.ci.portland.or.us/
parks/crysspringrhodgar.htm

For half a century, the Crystal Springs Rhododendron Garden has added splashes of vibrant spring and summer color to Crystal Springs Lake. Spanning seven acres on an island and peninsula in the spring-fed lake, the garden offers a series of surprises, with lagoons, bridges, waterfalls, and perennial beds tucked in along woodland paths. Surrounded by water and plenty of trees and shrubs that provide habitat and food, the garden is a *de facto* bird refuge. More than 100 species of birds—from great blue herons, to buffleheads, to American coots—have been observed in the garden. In 1950, the Portland Chapter of the American Rhododendron Society started a test garden on the island with support from the Portland Parks Department. Since then, dedicated volunteers, including society members and master gardeners, have planted and maintained the garden, often with plants donated from their own collections. It now includes more than 3,000 rhododendrons

Mossman's Freckles rhododendron at Crystal Springs

and azaleas, many of them rare species and hybrids that bloom from March through June. A new gatehouse invites visitors to follow a gently graded, paved path to the high bridge, a handsome, arched structure with Chippendale-style details. A path to the right of the bridge, along the north lagoon, leads to the new Elaine D. Flowerree waterfall garden, designed by Portland landscape architect Marlene Salon. Returning under the bridge, you enter the Jane Martin garden, featuring another waterfall. Beyond the high bridge is a lush overlook garden, once a mass of forbidding hollies, and now planted with azaleas, sedums, and Russian sage. Sturdy wooden benches here and elsewhere provide places to rest and observe waterfowl and other birds. At the south end of the peninsula, a low bridge connects the island and provides a view of the fountain in the south lagoon. A path around the edge of the lagoon leads to a rock garden with dianthus, coral bells, and yarrows, as well as tiny alpine rhododendrons and azaleas. Although dedicated to the rhododendron family, the garden displays colorful and interesting plants that extend the bloom season, such as pink and cantaloupe-colored Asian lilies, lacecap hydrangeas, and more than 100 different trees.

7 Portland: Leach Botanical Garden

LOCATION: SOUTHEAST CORNER OF PORTLAND, ON SE 122ND AVENUE NEAR SE FOSTER ROAD

GARDEN OPEN: 9am–4pm Tuesday-Saturday, 1–4pm Sunday
ADMISSION: Free
FURTHER INFORMATION FROM: 6704 SE 122nd Avenue Portland 97236.
503.761.9503

Located along meandering wooded paths on the banks of Johnson Creek, the Leach Botanical Garden is a testament to the enduring passion for plants that united Lilla and John Leach for nearly 60 years. Lilla Irvin Leach was a University of Oregon-trained botanist who delighted in searching for botanical treasures. John R. Leach, a local pharmacist and community leader, claimed he won Lilla's hand because he could lead a mule team into the rugged wilderness in search of plants. Married in 1913, they explored Oregon and Washington's mountain slopes together. Lilla discovered five new species of plants. The most remarkable find was in 1930 in Oregon's Siskiyou Mountains, when she spotted a rare, red-flowering, native shrub—*Kalmiopsis leachiana*—later named in her honor. (Her discovery led to the area's designation under federal protection as the Kalmiopsis Wilderness Area, the only place the plant was known to exist). In 1936, Lilla and John built their home, Sleepy Hollow, and created the original five-acre garden. By the late 1940s, they had given up expeditions, and for the next quarter-century devoted themselves to their garden. In 1972, they donated their land and life's work to the city of Portland to be enjoyed as a botanical museum. The estate was opened to the public in 1983 with the help of the Leach Garden Friends, which owns the property jointly with City of Portland Parks and Recreation. The garden has preserved and further developed the Leach's early collections, reflecting their eclectic tastes and love of native Northwest plants—woody groundcovers, viburnums, hollies, ferns, bamboo, trilliums, witch-hazels, and shrubs from the southeastern United States. With 16 acres and more than 2,000 different plant species, the garden's display of color extends beyond the springtime show of magnolias, dogwoods, camellias, and hepaticas. It includes plants with fall color and winter interest, such as stewartia, sugar maples, and katsura trees, whose golden-apricot leaves smell like burnt sugar as they fall. The brick entry garden and perennial beds around the house are accessible to garden lovers in wheelchairs. Up the sloped path north of the house is a rock garden with native sedums, eriogonums, and penstemons. A Northwest xeric habitat features a yellow iris (*Iris innominata*) discovered by Lilla Leach. A dry conifer forest of Douglas fir and red huckleberry provides habitat for local wildlife. Beyond it is a wildflower garden with snow queens, fawn lilies, and star-flowering Solomon's seal. The fern garden extends along the drive and down the stone steps to the creek, displaying hart's tongue ferns, holly ferns, and licorice ferns, as well as native maidenhair and deer ferns. Across the creek, a stone cabin the Leaches lived in before building their house features an inlaid marble floor from Italy that John had designed in honor of their anniversary, with "Lilla + John" inscribed in a tree design.

Native plants cascade down steps to the creek

8 Aloha: Jenkins Estate

LOCATION: OFF FARMINGTON ROAD AND SW 209TH AVENUE, 16 MILES WEST
OF PORTLAND

GARDEN OPEN: 8am–8pm
Monday–Thursday and
8am–4pm Friday, Memorial
Day through September;
8am–5pm Monday–Friday
October through May

ADMISSION: Free

FURTHER INFORMATION FROM:
8005 SW Grabhorn Road
Aloha 97007.
503.642.3855

Once known as Lolomi, an Indian word meaning "peace and quiet," the Jenkins Estate spreads out over 68 sloping acres of Cooper Mountain, overlooking the Tualatin Valley. From 1912 to 1915, Belle Ainsworth Jenkins, the daughter of a Portland shipping magnate and financier, and her husband, Ralph Jenkins, a station agent for the railroad, developed a country estate. Their love of horses had brought them together, and here they created a life around their avocations. They built a rustic main house styled like the British Royal family's hunting lodge, a carriage house, a stable, and riding arena—as well as splendid English-style gardens, a greenhouse, an ornamental pool, and a teahouse. The gar-

The Jenkins Estate fish pond

dens were planned by the gardener for the Prime Minister of Canada and planted in the English Picturesque style. There were miles of stone-lined pathways, and many specimen trees imported from around the world. In the early years, when the Jenkins entertained lavishly, plants bordered every path, and the estate employed 23 gardeners. During the last 30 years of her life, Belle ceased entertaining (her husband meanwhile enjoyed being driven to his club in the city every afternoon to play dominoes). From the mid-1960s to mid-1970s, in the years following their deaths, the estate was owned privately and became increasingly neglected; at one time, it was threatened by the development of a subdivision. After local voters approved a $10 million bond issue, however, the Tualatin Hills Park & Recreation District bought the estate in 1976 and began to restore the gardens with volunteer help from local gardeners. Many of the large trees of the Jenkins era—redwoods, European beech, Japanese maples—still stand, providing beautiful fall color. Beneath them, paths have been restored, and a rock garden buried under blackberry brambles was uncovered and replanted with heathers, columbine, azaleas, and native occidental rhododendrons. Perennial borders near the teahouse spill over with red day lilies. A rhododendron garden was added with more than 600 different varieties. Near a farmhouse on the property next to the original orchard, local garden clubs maintain an herb garden, rose arbors, and a Braille wall with markers for plants with interesting textures and fragrances such as lavender, scented geraniums, and lamb's ear sage. Though not as elaborate as they once were, the gardens of the Jenkins Estate are charming and recall the rustic but tasteful style of a more gracious era.

9 Silverton: The Oregon Garden

LOCATION: ONE MILE SOUTHWEST OF DOWNTOWN, AT 879 WEST MAIN STREET

Launching its preview season in the spring of 2000, The Oregon Garden promises a wide range of garden experiences on a grand scale. The garden is a joint venture between The Oregon Garden Foundation, a private nonprofit organization, and the City of Silverton, with the help of over 200 donors. Its mission is to construct a world-class public display garden, inspired by the Oregon Nurserymen's Association's dream of creating a showcase for the great richness of plants that grow well in the region. After a decade of planning, ground was broken in 1997 on a city-owned site that was formerly an Arabian horse breeding ranch. The first phase of construction spans 60 acres and includes formal gardens, an amphitheater, wetlands,

GARDEN OPEN: 10am–6pm daily in summer, 10am–3pm daily in winter
ADMISSION: Free while under construction during 2000
FURTHER INFORMATION FROM: PO Box 155 Silverton 97381-0155. 503.874.8100

TOP: *Oregon Garden from the air*
BOTTOM: *The wetlands*

and an arboretum setting. The A-mazing Water Garden combines a maze-like water feature traversing a slope with an innovative biological system of recycling city water. Instead of being dumped into a local creek after it goes through a water treatment plant, the "gray" water from Silverton's homes and businesses will be pumped to The Oregon Garden. The nitrogen–rich water, ideal for irrigating plants, will circulate through the water garden, cleansed further by some 300,000 aquatic plants including water lilies. A master plan calls for the garden to eventually encompass more than 200 acres, with views of the Willamette Valley and individual gardens such as an axis garden, a sensory garden, and a children's garden. The Silverton Garden, for example, will focus on the agricultural history of the valley, growing hops, grapes, berries, and hazelnuts.

10 Salem: Bush's Pasture Park

LOCATION: IN DOWNTOWN SALEM, AT THE INTERSECTION OF MISSION AND
HIGH STREETS

Bush's Pasture Park encompasses about 75 acres of open
spaces, walking paths, a playground, and an arts center located
in the barn of what was once the estate of Ashahel Bush, pioneer banker and newspaperman. The park's glory, however, is
its gardens, especially its roses, which comprise the
Northwest's finest public collection of old roses. Native Garry
oaks tower over the circa-1877 Victorian home, now a house
museum. Beneath them are tulip and annual beds that recall
the Victorian penchant for "bedding out" with colorful flowers
in complex, symmetrical patterns. West of the barn is a large
perennial garden with dozens of peonies. In its heyday, the
Bush estate included a Japanese garden, tennis court, and a
glass conservatory that Ashahel built for his daughter Sally, an
avid gardener who supplied her father's bank with fresh bouquets. The conservatory—the second oldest in the West—still
stands, covered with summer-blooming scented clematis.
Before it is a garden of herbs popular during the Victorian era.
The city bought the Bush property in 1953, and two years later
the parks department created the hybrid-tea rose garden, which
includes many no longer available in North America. They
bloom in every conceivable color and fragrance, planted in
numbered beds in a formal pattern of rectangles and wedges
appropriate to the Victorian era. Beds 80 through 83 surrounding the gazebo are called "Miss Sally's Garden" and contain the

GARDEN OPEN: Dawn to dusk
daily

ADMISSION: Free

FURTHER INFORMATION FROM:
Salem Art Association,
Bush Barn
600 Mission Street, SE
Salem 97302.
503.581.2228

NEARBY SIGHTS OF INTEREST:
Historic Deepwood Estate

*The rose garden Bush's
Pasture Park is known for,
with the garden's 1877
Victorian house in the
background*

original Bush collection of older roses such as Dainty Bess and Golden Ophelia, hybrid teas from 1925 and 1918, respectively. Just west of it is the Tartar Collection, named after Mae Tartar, who in 1960 donated her collection of old roses originally brought from the East by early pioneers. They include some mentioned in ancient literature—gallicas such as the Apothecary's Rose and Rosa Mundi, as well as Bella Donna, a pre-1844, fragrant pink damask rose. Screened with beautiful trees and shrubs, this garden was designed earlier by Elizabeth Lord and Edith Schryver, friends of the Bushes who became renowned as the region's first landscape architecture firm run by women. Lord and Schryver were so fond of the Bush estate that even into the 1950s, well on in years, they hauled wonderful trees here in their old Hudson and commandeer the city gardener to plant them. The result decades later is a beautifully colored and textured setting for the outstanding collections of historic roses.

11 Salem: Historic Deepwood Estate

LOCATION: IN DOWNTOWN SALEM, AT CORNER OF 12TH AND MISSION

GARDEN OPEN: Dawn to dusk daily
TOURS OF HOUSE : noon–5pm hourly, Sunday-Friday; May–September and Tuesday–Saturday in October
ADMISSION: Free; tours of house $4 adults, $3 students and seniors, $2 children 6-12, children under 6 free
FURTHER INFORMATION FROM: 1116 Mission Street, SE Salem 97302.
503.363.1825
www.oregonlink.com/deep-wood/
NEARBY SIGHTS OF INTEREST: Bush's Pasture Park

A lusciously extravagant perennial border nearly a block long greets visitors to the Historic Deepwood Estate. Deep drifts of color flow from cool to warm and to cool again—white phlox and pink butterfly bushes to apricot climbing roses and red dahlias, to daisies and lamb's ear. The Volunteer Deepwood Gardeners designed this border—with inspiration from the designs and color theories of the great English garden designer Gertrude Jekyll—as an alluring entry to Deepwood's two-and-a-half acres of English-style gardens. The gardens were designed in 1929 by innovative landscape architects Elizabeth Lord and Edith Schryver, the Northwest's first firm of professionally trained women landscape architects. Lord–Schryver were known for planning successions of blooms, organizing outdoor "rooms" as extensions of the house, and creating a sense of charm through numerous small-scale enclosures. Listed on the National Register of Historic Places, Deepwood Estate is their most widely recognized garden and their only residential garden open to the public. Recently widowed Alice Brown hired the team in 1929, and over the next 16 years, they designed and planted gardens around the 1894 Queen Anne-style home, designed by architect W.C. Knighton. After Alice's death in 1970, Deepwood was purchased by the city of Salem and since 1974 has been managed by the Friends of Deepwood. Lord–Schryver's design focused on the west, south, and east sides of the house. The great room, the first garden completed in 1936, has the grand-

The perennial border next to Alice Brown's Queen Anne-style home

est scale, with a north-south axis, boxwood hedges, and a wrought-iron gazebo from Portland's 1905 Lewis and Clark Exposition. A pergola to the east covered with grapes, roses, and clematis leads into the spring garden, a more informal space planted with peonies, poppies, and roses. The tea garden is an intricate, intimate design with an east-west axis and brick crosspaths. Boxwood-edged beds brim with fragrant herbs and flowers such as lilies, phlox, roses, and bee balm. We can easily imagine Alice's guests, wearing garden hats and white gloves, seated in the green gazebo or on the covered benches, sipping tea and chatting. (Behind the gazebo and a holly hedge are a greenhouse and the entrance to three acres of graveled nature trails). An ivy arbor to the west leads to the lower terrace's scroll garden, the site of Alice's second marriage to Keith Powell in 1945. It is embellished with scrolls, from the intricate, cinnabar-colored iron fence, to the yew hedges, to Schryver's trademark S-shaped boxwood plantings. On the west side of the house is the family's backyard, a more informal space with a gazebo and garden ornaments such as a classical stone column from the ruins of the 1876 Oregon statehouse. A boxwood hedge screens a secret garden next to the solarium (the intimate proportions of the garden are best appreciated from the porch above). We can imagine Alice in her refuge writing to Lord and Schryver, "You've made it beautifully...I'll never be satisfied just to have it please one's eye—it must stir the imagination—or it is no real garden."

Roses climb the barn in the perennial border at Historic Deepwood Estate

12 Eugene: Owen Rose Garden

LOCATION: ON THE WILLAMETTE RIVER, AT THE NORTH END OF JEFFERSON STREET, OFF 1ST AVENUE.

Located on the Willamette River, with benches and picnic tables throughout the grounds and paths that connect to a riverfront bike path, the Owen Rose Garden is a wonderful place to relax and smell the roses. The rose garden, which encompasses about five of the park's eight acres, is an All-American Rose Selection (AARS) accredited public display garden. It features more than 4,500 roses in borders and formal and informal beds, including varieties such as hybrid teas, floribundas, grandifloras, climbers, miniatures, and polyanthas. Thousands of roses of every hue bloom during the peak season, usually the second and third weeks in June. Many others bloom throughout the summer and early fall. Year-round color is captured in

GARDEN OPEN: 6am–11pm daily

ADMISSION: Free

FURTHER INFORMATION FROM: City of Eugene Parks Maintenance 1820 Roosevelt Boulevard Eugene 97402. 541.682.4800

NEARBY SIGHTS OF INTEREST: Hendricks Park and Rhododendron Garden

spring bulbs, spring and summer annuals and perennials, and shrubs and trees. A recent addition is beds of Japanese iris that were donated to the city by Eugene's sister city, Kakegawa, Japan. The garden's most striking tree is a black Republican cherry believed to be the largest cherry tree in Oregon and one of the largest in the United States. A remnant of an early riverfront orchard, the tree dates to 1847. In the past century, George Owen, a local lumberman, philanthropist, and city councilor, and his wife, Enid, developed the land as a riverfront estate. In 1950, the Owens donated to the city both the land around their home and matching funds to develop it as a park. Following some behind-the-scenes lobbying from the Eugene Rose Society, Enid Owen convinced her husband that some of the land should be devoted to a municipal rose garden. The rose society was instrumental in designing and planting the rose gardens, and its members contributed 750 plants for the original collection. The city recently began a restoration and new development project with funds from the Eugene Delta Rotary Club and volunteers from garden clubs. The project focuses on the bones of the garden—new arbors and pathways, wooden borders for beds, a trellis along the west side of the park, water features, a gazebo, and pergolas over the walkway from the parking lot.

GARDEN OPEN: 6am–11pm daily

TOURS: Sundays in April and May at 1pm

ADMISSION: Free

FURTHER INFORMATION FROM:
1800 Skyline Boulevard
Eugene 97403.
541.682.5324

NEARBY SIGHTS OF INTEREST:
Owen Rose Garden, Mount Pisgah Arboretum

13 Eugene: Hendricks Park and Rhododendron Garden

LOCATION: SUMMIT AND SKYLINE DRIVES, OFF FAIRMONT BOULEVARD

Set on a hillside, the 12-acre Rhododendron Garden encompasses nearly 6,000 woody ornamental plants within Hendricks Park's 78 acres. Some 3,500 rhododendrons and azaleas comprise the garden's most significant collection. In 1906, Martha and Thomas Hendricks, realizing "the necessity to procure such a park at the present time while it was available in its natural state," purchased 47 acres of forested ridgeline and gave it to the city of Eugene, which bought an adjoining tract of 31 acres and dedicated the property as Hendricks Park. In 1951, members of the Eugene chapter of the American Rhododendron Society founded the Rhododendron Garden and donated their own collections of species and hybrids. One area, for example, is dedicated to James Barto, who between 1925 and his death in 1940, cultivated on his farm the largest and most outstanding collection of rhododendron species in the United States. Many plants from his collection are included here, such as the smoky purple-blooming *Rhododendron ririei* and the 25-foot Beauty of Littleworth. Though the garden's name suggests rhododendrons are its only claim to fame, an extensive collection of trees, shrubs, and herbaceous plants provide year-round interest. Thanks to the region's mild, almost Mediterranean climate—and the generosity of a nationally known local nursery—the garden has perhaps the best collection of magnolias of any public garden on the West Coast—over 200 trees of 60 different varieties. The garden displays rich layers, including a canopy of native Oregon white oaks and Douglas fir, an understory of magnolias and dogwoods, flowering shrubs such as virburnums and witch hazels, and herbaceous plants such as ferns, bulbs, and perennials. Meandering gravel paths allow you to wander through this luxuriant landscape, and seating areas encourage meditation near the garden's many small waterfalls and fountains.

14 Eugene: Mount Pisgah Arboretum

LOCATION: WITHIN THE HOWARD BUFORD RECREATION AREA, FIVE MILES SOUTHEAST OF EUGENE

GARDEN OPEN: Dawn to dusk daily

ADMISSION: Free

FURTHER INFORMATION FROM: Friends of the Mount Pisgah Arboretum
33735 Seavey Loop Road
Eugene 97405.
541.747.3817 or 541.741.4110

NEARBY SIGHTS OF INTEREST: Hendricks Park and Rhododendron Garden, Owen Rose Garden

Mount Pisgah Arboretum is a bucolic 208-acre garden within the 2,300-acre Howard Buford Recreation Area, a Lane County park bordering the Coast Fork of the Willamette River. Located on the slope of Mount Pisgah, the site was formerly hunting grounds for the Calapooia Indians and later a pioneer farm. From high points on the trails, there are spectacular views of the Willamette Valley and Coast Range. The arboretum is a living museum with an amazing diversity of ecosystems that allow for the display of many native Willamette Valley trees, shrubs, wildflowers, and wild creatures. Seven miles of groomed nature trails pass through these distinct plant communities and ecosystems. The intermittent stream, its banks bearing Oregon ash, carries water from the upper reaches of 1,520-foot Mount Pisgah on its way to the Pacific. Oregon white oaks rise from the oak savanna's meadows. The mixed conifer forest features the Northwest's signature Douglas fir trees, and the upper plateau blooms with Pacific native dogwood. The seasonal marsh is dry in summer, but wet and boggy in spring, when it is lush with yellow monkey flower. Near the end of the trail, aromatic resins from a grove of towering incense cedars perfume the air. When the state purchased the land and later deeded it to the county 30 years ago, the site was overgrown with poison oak and impenetrable ten-foot blackberry thickets that engulfed trees and hid the river from the great meadow. During the first five years, arboretum members, volunteers, and CETA crews cleared dilapidated farm buildings and began the long process of eradicating blackberries and poison oak. Since 1973, a private nonprofit organization now known as the

Miles of paths wind through meadows and woods at Mt. Pisgah Arboretum

Friends of Mount Pisgah Arboretum has overseen construction of the trail system, some 20 bridges, and individual garden areas, such as the one devoted to wildflowers. Supported almost entirely by private donations and volunteers, the arboretum conducts an extensive education program, including an outdoor science program for local elementary school students.

GARDEN OPEN: 8 am–sunset daily

ADMISSION: $3 daily parking fee

FURTHER INFORMATION FROM: Sunset Bay Management Unit 89814 Cape Arago Highway Coos Bay 97420. 541.888.3732

NEARBY SIGHTS OF INTEREST: Sunset Bay State Park, Cape Arago State Park

15 Coos Bay: Shore Acres Gardens

LOCATION: ON CAPE ARAGO HIGHWAY, 13 MILES SW OF NORTH BEND AND COOS BAY AND U.S. HIGHWAY 101

On a scenic bluff high above the Pacific Ocean, Shore Acres is a historic private estate garden turned state park. It began in 1905 as a 745-acre estate, purchased by lumber baron and shipbuilder Louis B. Simpson as a Christmas gift for his wife. Simpson built a showcase summer home—a three-story mansion with a ballroom, indoor pool, and five acres of formal gardens including, boxwood-trimmed geometric beds, expanses of manicured lawn, a garden house, a greenhouse, and a Japanese-style garden built around a 100-foot lily pond. Flowering plants, shrubs, and trees brought from around the world on Simpson-owned sailing ships filled the gardens. A fire destroyed the mansion in 1921, and Simpson began to build an even larger replacement. Financial losses in the 1930s, however, caused the house and grounds to fall into disrepair, and in 1942, Simpson sold the estate to the State of Oregon for use as a public park. The deteriorating mansion was eventually razed, and an observation building was built in its place on the bluff, with views of rugged seascapes and migrating whales. Beginning in the mid-1970s, the gardens were restored with boxwood-bordered beds following the original layout, an Oriental garden and pond, and 900 rose bushes in several different gardens (the presence of roses is all the more remarkable because of the site's often cool, damp, windy conditions and acidic clay.) The collections include old garden roses such as La Reine Victoria, species roses, and an All-American Rose Selections display garden with award winners such as Gemini, a hybrid tea with double coral and cream-colored blossoms and dark green foliage. The mild climate allows for year-round displays, from thousands of flowering bulbs in early spring, to rhododendrons and azaleas in late spring, to perennials and roses in summer, and dahlias that bloom into October. Evergreen shrubs and trees, including Oregon's largest Monterey pine, provide winter color and help set the stage for the annual "holiday lights" festival from Thanksgiving through the New Year. In addition to the seven acres of formal gardens, the grounds cover 738 acres of naturalized areas. A hiking trail connects Shore Acres with camping and picnic facilities one mile to the north, at Sunset Bay State Park, and with more trails, tide-pools, and marine mammal viewing one mile to the south at Cape Arago State Park.

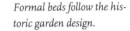

Formal beds follow the historic garden design.

PORT MADISON BAY

THE GLEN

MAIN ENTRANCE

PARKING

ORCHID TRAIL

EAST BLUFF

FERN HILL

MOSS GARDEN

JAPANESE GARDEN

FIR HILL

REFLECTION GARDEN

THE WOODS

BOARDWALK

TRESTLE BRIDGE

BIRD REFUGE

16 Bainbridge Island: The Bloedel Reserve

LOCATION: TAKE SEATTLE-WINSLOW FERRY FROM SEATTLE OR AGATE PASS
BRIDGE FROM OLYMPIC PENINSULA; ROUTE 305 TO DOLPHIN DRIVE

GARDEN OPEN: 10 am–4 pm
Wednesday–Sunday, by
advance reservation only
ADMISSION: $6, $4 seniors
and ages 5-12, children under
5 free
FURTHER INFORMATION FROM:
7571 NE Dolphin Drive
Bainbridge Island 98110-1097.
206.842.7631
www.bloedelreserve.org

Across Puget Sound from Seattle, on a quiet bay on the northeast tip of Bainbridge Island, lies the Bloedel Reserve, a garden estate, arboretum, and nature preserve that recalls the halcyon days of an earlier era. Spread out across 150 acres, the reserve is a study in contrasts. Huge sweeps of pastureland are open to the sky, and more than half its acreage is undeveloped forest. Part pristine natural landscape and part exquisitely designed estate, the reserve is blessed with a favorable climate and conditions for growing a diversity of plants, both native and exotic. The reserve's primary interest is the relationship between plants and people, and it is meant as a place where people can find refreshment and tranquility in the presence of natural beauty. It is a place apart, and a morning or afternoon of attentive ambling is certain balm for garden lovers whose daily pace may seem stuck on fast-forward. Because the reserve is careful about preserving the landscape's sense of quietude, it reserves spaces for a limited number of visitors at scheduled intervals. Once you're there, you may stay as long as you would like until closing.

The land has long been valued as a retreat. Angela Collins purchased part of the property in 1904 as a beach retreat, and in 1931 built the French chateau-style home, now the visitor center, on a bluff overlooking the sound. In 1950, Prentice and Virginia Bloedel purchased 67 of the original acres after Prentice retired as vice president of a lumber company he helped establish in Canada. The Bloedels added to the house and built a garage and a Japanese-style guesthouse. They also added 83 acres to their property and in 1954 began to develop the landscape. Over the next 35 years, with the assistance of many gifted landscape architects and garden designers, they created formal gardens influenced by European and Asian traditions, and informal gardens, such as a glen, a bog, a waterfall garden, and an orchid trail, that emphasized the beauty of the natural landscape. The Bloedels gave 100 acres of their property to the University of Washington in 1970, and in 1974, The Arbor Fund was established to manage them. The Fund purchased the property in 1986, opened the Bloedel Reserve to the public in 1989, and continues to manage it and interpret the Bloedels' vision.

The gatehouse, echoing the style of the main house, establishes the tone for the reserve: dignified, understated, and elegant. Inside you'll find a map of the Reserve, as well as advice from knowledgeable docents about plants in bloom. A Western

OPPOSITE: *Trestle Bridge on trail between the bird marsh and the central garden*

123

red cedar stands sentry in the large west meadow where Virginia Bloedel's sheep once grazed. A path curves past storage barns that held Prentice's prized old-growth cedar logs, which were eventually used to fence part of the property. A soft wood-mulch path enters the woods, a dense Northwest forest dominated by Douglas firs, Western red cedars, and hemlocks. Dappled sunlight illuminates understory plants such as foxglove, mahonia, rhododendrons, and salal. The path descends to the bird refuge. Here ducks, geese, and trumpeter swans paddle among the sedges, and tiny islands dot the pond. Red-winged blackbirds roost on the cattails in spring, and great blue heron, kingfishers, and eagles regularly dive for trout. Red osier dogwood, winterberry, western azaleas, spirea, and moosewood viburnums provide natural screening and food and habitat for the birds.

A trestle bridge allows views into the forest floor. Benches and railings here are made of Jarrah wood (*Eucalyptus marginata*), noted for its resistance to rot and insect damage. Further on, the trail winds to the heart of the forest, past old stumps and mossy logs, to forest wetlands and the headwaters of a year-round stream. A boardwalk leads across the bog, thick with red alders, lady ferns, and a few carnivorous pitcher plants. The path converges with the driveway to the house. Gracing the drive are beautiful trees and shrubs, including a Persian parrot tree with brilliant fall color and weeping willow and Young's weeping birch across the pond. Japanese maples, gorgeous blue lacecap hydrangeas, heathers, and ornamental grasses gather beside the stream that connects to a second pond where tundra swans swim. Flanking the house are two huge English elms (*Ulmus procera*) and an empress tree (*Paulownia tomentosa*) that blooms in June with large lavender trumpet flowers. In 1979, the bluff on the east side of the house was lowered 15 feet and reshaped by landscape architect Richard Haag to take advantage of the view of Puget Sound. The curving pattern of turf

grasses was designed by Geoffrey Rausch. Thomas Church, another gifted landscape architect and a long-time friend and landscape advisor to the Bloedels, designed the bluff patio, which features a boxwood hedge and two beautifully spreading camperdown elms planted by Angela Collins.

A new granite staircase overlooks a waterfall and leads down into the glen, where rhododendrons thrive under the protection of second-growth timber, along with stands of Himalayan white birch, Japanese maples, and wildflowers and bulbs including 15,000 cyclamen. The orchid trail, originally laid out by Thomas Church, features a small garden designed by Geoffrey Rausch, composed of fragrant native azaleas, trilliums, and western rhododendrons. A catalpa tree and a white Kousa dogwood mark the gate to the Japanese garden that surrounds the guest house. A graceful hybrid of Japanese teahouse and Pacific Northwest Indian longhouse, the guesthouse was designed in 1964 by Seattle architect Paul Hayden Kirk. Built in 1960-61 by Fujitaro Kubota, the Japanese stroll garden that surrounds the pond directs the eye to many views, while the stone and sand meditation garden, designed by Koichi Kawana, suggests introspection. Handsome trees punctuate the landscape, including a lace-leaf maple more than 140 years old and red and black pines, representing the female and male elements of the garden. The color black is repeated in details such as twine that joins the fencing and the black foliage of the lily turf that borders the stone path. The use of black in Japanese gardens represents handiwork worthy of a higher order because black traditionally has been a difficult (and therefore expensive) color to obtain from natural sources.

Created in 1982, the moss garden is a luxuriously soft, intensely green and velvety carpet that covers huge stumps and gnarled trunks. To achieve this hushed woodland chapel, 2,200 flats of Irish moss (*Sagina subulata*) were brought in and divided into 275,000 starts, which were planted six inches apart beneath the large leaves of Hercules walking stick trees. Beyond the moss garden, enclosed by a yew hedge, is the 200-foot-long reflecting pool, an exercise in design simplicity that compels viewers to ruminate beyond the mere physical space. A wooded path lined with woodpoppies, white violets, and Grecian windflowers leads back to the west meadow. Re-emerging into the sunlight and golden grasses, I was reluctant to leave. A few hours at Bloedel Reserve reminded me of Prentice Bloedel's often-expressed belief that "nature does not need us to survive, but we need nature in order to connect with a sense of creation."

OPPOSITE, TOP: *Entry to moss garden*
OPPOSITE, BOTTOM: *Autumn at the Japanese pool. Tall conifer in the center is a Serbian Spruce.*
BELOW: *Woodland ravine garden—just west of Christmas Pool*
BOTTOM: *Spring skunk flowers at the Japanese pool*

GARDEN OPEN: By appointment on Thursday, Friday, and Saturday April 1st–September 30

ADMISSION: $7 includes guided tour discount for seniors; no pets or children under 12

FURTHER INFORMATION FROM:
The E.B. Dunn Historic
Garden Trust
PO Box 77126
Seattle 98177.
206.362.0933

17 Seattle: The Dunn Garden

LOCATION: NORTHWEST SEATTLE

A leisurely stroll around the grounds of the Dunn Garden can give the amazing effect of being in a time warp. The seven-acre garden, located on a bluff in a quiet, exclusive, residential area of the city overlooking Puget Sound, is a snapshot of the elegant yet relaxed garden-design style of a generation ago. The beautifully scaled garden spaces and richly layered plantings, including many mature trees and shrubs, recall an even earlier time, when the landscape surrounding the three Dunn homes was one estate. In 1915, the Olmsted Brothers, landscape architects *par excellence*, designed the site as a summer estate for the Arthur Dunn family. Dunn moved to Seattle from upstate New York and missed the East's vivid fall colors, so the Olmsteds designed the property, which had been clear cut, to include a (now-mature) canopy of sugar maples, oaks, beeches, tulip trees, and magnolias that is unusually brilliant for a Northwest garden. Though in the 1940s the grounds were divided among three separate residences, the Dunn family retained the landscape's unifying ideals of naturalistic groupings of trees set amidst broad lawns and flowering borders of shrubs and groundcovers. Within this context, the Dunn family began to create their own gardens. Edward B. Dunn, Arthur's son, loved plants, especially rhododendrons. He was a president of the American Rhododendron Society in the late 1950s, and a founder of the Rhododendron Species Foundation. He knew all the leading rhododendron hybridizers, who gave him various unnamed plants. Ed actively gardened until he was in his late 70s. After he died in 1991 at 87, the family established the E.B. Dunn Historic Garden Trust to continue his legacy. Since then, the trust has taken on numerous restoration projects, including thinning out and replanting Ed's lovely woodland garden. Once the site of the original garage and kitchen garden, this two-and-a-half-acre garden is rich with dogwoods, trilliums, and avalanche lilies beneath Douglas fir, chestnuts, and maples. A grassy path meanders through a glen, past a moss garden, a waterfall and a stream, to a glade bordered with perennial flowers and benches. The great lawn, a central feature of the original estate, provides a view of Puget Sound. The great lawn blooms in spring with thousands of crocuses. Its perimeter is graced with individual gardens, such as a heather berm and a perennial border. A wildflower glen with foxglove and lilies leads to a woodland trail with narcissus, alliums, and hydrangeas. The "tennis court garden"—

Dunn Garden House

its name suggests its intended former life—is rimmed with variegated dogwoods, cherry trees, and a spring border. Recent renovation of Ed's perennial border, on the north edge of his lawn, features seven-foot Himalayan lilies. Pathways, lawns, and woodland areas flow seamlessly from one group of plantings to the next, linked by textures, colors, and lines that create a sense of movement.

18 Seattle: Carl S. English, Jr. Botanical Garden

LOCATION: NW 54TH ST, NEAR THE INTERSECTION OF NW MARKET STREET

On its own, the Carl S. English, Jr. Botanical Garden would be a lovely attraction in Northwest Seattle. But given its proximity to the drama of boats passing through the Hiram M. Chittenden Locks that join Lakes Union and Washington with Puget Sound, they fall into the category of a fascinating garden experience. The U.S. Army Corps of Engineers opened the locks in 1916 and still maintain the site and the gardens within it. Displays along the concrete walkway explain how the locks work to transport sailboats and motorboats from one level to the next through the passage. To their delight, many visitors are drawn into the historic formal gardens that lead to the locks and are laid out around the Federal-style concrete administration building. The seven-acre garden features more than 1,500 plants, many of them original specimens that botanist Carl S. English, Jr., gathered from around the world between 1933 and 1974. Major collections include dogwoods, cherry trees, magnolias, rhododendrons, oaks, gingkoes, and maples, as well as specimen trees such as Chinese witch hazels and stewartias. Red horse chestnuts line the west side of the long walkway from the entrance, past the visitor center's beds of flowers and shrubs, to a fuchsia garden in front of the administration building. To the left are central rose beds with arbors of climbing roses, surrounded by perennial borders with anemones, delphiniums, and butterfly bush. In an adjacent formal garden, a perennial bed filled with hot-colored flowers such as scarlet bee balm and orange crocosmia is surrounded by lawn with borders of cooler colors such as daisies and sea lavender. On a summer evening, when the colors soften, and you can hear the boats cruising through the locks and smell the salt air, these gardens are simply enchanting.

GARDEN OPEN: 7am–9pm daily

ADMISSION: Free

FURTHER INFORMATION FROM:
Hiram M. Chittenden Locks
3015 NW 54th Street
Seattle 98107.
206.783.7059
www.nws.usace.army.mil/opd
iv/lwsc

NEARBY SIGHTS OF INTEREST:
Hiram M. Chittenden Locks

"Lucifer" crocosmia

GARDEN OPEN: Dawn to dusk daily

ADMISSION: Free ($3.50 to park at zoo)

FURTHER INFORMATION FROM:
Woodland Park Zoo
5500 Phinney Avenue North
Seattle 98103.
206.684.4800 or 4863
www.zoo.org

NEARBY SIGHTS OF INTEREST:
Woodland Park Zoo

19 Seattle: Woodland Park Rose Garden

LOCATION: AT THE WOODLAND PARK ZOO, ON PHINNEY AVENUE, AT N 50TH AND FREEMONT AVENUE NORTH

Woodland Park has perhaps the prettiest rose garden in Seattle, filled with fragrant roses, topiary, and a classically inspired reflecting pool that sets the stage perfectly for the weddings that frequently take place here. Woodland Park began with Guy Phinney, a Seattle real estate tycoon, who purchased 188 acres near the south shores of Green Lake and developed his personal estate, including a mansion, formal gardens, and a private zoo. After his death in 1883, the City of Seattle purchased the estate and hired the Olmsted Brothers firm from Brookline, Massachusetts, to design Woodland Park (though they did not design the rose garden). The zoo, officially established in 1899, is home to 1,000 animals that live among plants appropriate to six bioclimatic zones, such as an orchid-draped tropical rain forest. Next to the zoo, which charges admission, is a two-and-a-half-acre formal rose garden, fenced with Victorian wrought iron, stone pillars, and elaborate gates. The rose garden was established in 1924, and is an official All-American Rose Selections test garden, with more than 5,000 roses of 283 varieties. What makes it so marvelous is its design. Entering the west gate, you find a symmetrical design of architectural features on axis, surrounded by geometrical and curvilinear beds and borders. A central planter (formerly a fountain), encircled with dogwoods, lavender, lilies, and mossy thyme, is flanked on four corners by large topiary Sawara cypress (*Chamaecyparis pisifera squarrosa*). Sculpted into wildly knobby, undulating, almost grotesque shapes, these evergreens stand guard over precious specimens such as Midas Touch gold hybrid tea roses. Further east are a gazebo and arbors, separated by a perennial border with delphiniums and vermilion Sarabande floribundas. To the south of the central planter are two long boxwood-bordered beds and yew "gumdrops" enclosing a bed of white and red roses. Diaphanous baby's breath surrounds tree roses in other beds. At the garden's north end is a reflecting pool with an all-white garden and a view beyond to a white classical bas relief. Especially at dawn or dusk, this dreamy scene is straight out of a Maxfield Parish painting. Bordered by creamy hedge roses and hybrid rugosa roses, the reflecting pool is animated by white water lilies, shimmering koi, and fountain spray. The bas relief is dedicated to the garden's founders, the Seattle Rose Society and the Lion's Club. Serpentine beds of amber-colored floribundas snake their way back to the grand west gate.

Topiary yews and gazebo

20 # Seattle: The Medicinal Herb Garden

LOCATION: ON THE UNIVERSITY OF WASHINGTON CAMPUS, AT 15TH AVENUE
NE AND NE 40TH STREET

Located within the heart of an urban campus, the Medicinal
Herb Garden comprises two serene acres of herbaceous plants
used for ornament, domestic purposes, and traditional medicine—perhaps the largest collection of its kind in the Western
Hemisphere. The historic garden is used to train students of
pharmacology, botany, landscape architecture, urban horticulture, art, and anthropology. Established on one acre in 1911 by
the University of Washington School of Pharmacology, it was
expanded during World War I to help offset a critical national
shortage of belladonna, digitalis, and other natural drugs. By
1942, the gardens filled eight acres and five greenhouses with
hundreds of different kinds of plants from around the world. In
more recent decades, the garden was redesigned, scaled down,
and, in the 1980s, restored by a volunteer group, the Friends of
the Medicinal Herb Garden. It is now laid out in a series of garden "rooms" with both formal beds and informal borders richly
planted with trees and shrubs. Cascara Circle, a grassy glen
ringed by cascara trees and cut through by a slender runnel
"stream," contains a collection of regional plants once used by
native Americans and immigrating settlers for food and healing. The lower west garden's formal beds, filled with giant fennel, hollyhocks, and white baneberry, are framed by a mixed
hedge tapestry of tea, tall Oregon grape, and rockrose. Four 15-
foot Irish yews rise like classical columns to frame a view of
gothic stone buildings to the southeast. In the upper west garden grow popular herbs such as tobacco and goldenrod, contained by a border of boxwood, bay laurel, a great fig tree, and
peonies. A sunny central garden area features a rock seating
wall bordered by gingko trees, mock oranges, and viburnums
overlooking beds of showy cardinal flower, Mexican sunflowers, tall red penstemons, clary sage, and
Joe Pye weed. Two additional garden
rooms are bordered by a woodland area
and on the south by spreading hawthorn
trees and evergreen privet, holly, and bay
laurel hedges. A massive rosemary planting joins the two rooms and their displays
of culinary and medicinal herbs, such as
Greek oregano, caraway, Chinese pink bal-
loonflower (*Di-huang)* and sacred datura
with creamy white trumpet flowers.

GARDEN OPEN: Dawn to dusk
daily

ADMISSION: Free

FURTHER INFORMATION FROM:
Friends of the Medicinal Herb
Garden
Botany Department
Box 355325
University of Washington
Seattle 98195-5325.
206.543.1126
www.nnlm.nlm.nih.gov/pnr/u
wmhg

NEARBY SIGHTS OF INTEREST:
University of Washington
campus

*Perennial flowers and herbs
with borrowed scenery of a
gothic building*

GARDEN OPEN: 7am–dusk
daily

FURTHER INFORMATION FROM:
2300 Arboretum Drive East
Seattle 98112.
206.543.8800
http://depts.washington.edu/wpa

NEARBY SIGHTS OF INTEREST:
Japanese Garden of
Washington Park Arboretum

21 # Seattle: Washington Park Arboretum

LOCATION: IN EASTERN SEATTLE, JUST SOUTH OF LAKE WASHINGTON'S UNION BAY

Washington Park Arboretum's 230 rolling acres afford a pastoral escape within minutes of downtown Seattle. As one of the largest and most beautiful green spaces in the Puget Sound region, the arboretum is a well-loved park, popular with plant lovers, dog-walkers, bicyclists (on paved roads only), families with children, and caffeine-fueled Seattleites seeking a shady lawn to relax on. The collection of 10,000 trees and woody plants was founded on a smaller scale at the University of Washington in 1899. In 1934, the university and the City of Seattle agreed to locate the arboretum in Washington Park, and retained the Olmsted Brothers to design the first master plan. The arboretum is still operated and maintained cooperatively by the city and the university, with support from the Arboretum Foundation. This urban forest demonstrates the wealth of landscape plants suitable for the region. It is the largest public garden north of San Francisco and one of two prominent woody plant collections in the country, containing more than 5,500 different kinds of plants with collections devoted to mountain ashes, camellias, and other trees and shrubs. Individual gardens are strung like jewels along the trails of the arboretum, a long, narrow site that stretches south from Union Bay. The Azalea Way is a three-quarter-mile promenade lined with flowering

Loderi Valley path

cherries, dogwoods, and azaleas. Rhododendron Glen features species and hybrids, from dwarfs to trees, as well as companion plants such as gorgeous blue lacecap hydrangeas that bloom in August. From the Graham Visitor Center, a handsome building with wisteria-draped pergolas, it is a short stroll across a historic footbridge to the pinetum, a strange and wonderful collection of conifers, such as the monkey puzzle tree with slender branches and tiny armor-like "spikes." Just across from the visitor center, you'll find the J. A. Witt Winter Garden, a lovely collection named for a former curator of the arboretum. Here are evergreens and plants with interesting barks and berries that are not only handsome but feed wildlife during winter months, such as heathers, stewartias, hollies, and paper-bark maples. Nearby is the woodland garden, ravishing in the fall with crabapples, Pacific madroñas with smooth, peeling, reddish bark, and more than 170 cultivars of Japanese maples. A trail heading north from the visitor center leads to Foster Island, a waterfront area rife with waterfowl on the edge of Union Bay.

22 Seattle: Japanese Garden of Washington Park Arboretum

LOCATION: AT THE SOUTHERN TIP OF WASHINGTON PARK ARBORETUM

Washington Park's Japanese Garden is one of the most authentic to be found outside of Japan. Conceived over a twenty-year period, the three-and-a-half-acre garden was finally built in 1960. An exquisite stroll garden of the formal *shin* type, it was designed in the sixteenth-century Momoyama style by Juki Iida, one of Japan's "national treasures." Mr. Iida, who designed and built more than 1,000 Japanese gardens worldwide, directed the placement of more than 500 huge granite boulders ranging from 1,000 pounds to 11 tons that he selected from the Cascade Mountains. His plan included thousands of plants representing diverse scenes in Japan, including azaleas, rhododendrons, camellias, evergreens, flowering fruit trees, mosses, and ferns. A tour of the garden begins at the south gate (self-guiding brochures are available, as are cassette tapes). Take the east path past the *Ginkgo bilobas* and a carpet of moss to the lake, where you may see turtles sunning themselves on a small island. The pines on the island symbolize Japanese cranes. At the north end of the garden, a wisteria trellis marks the entrance to the "village," next to a stream planted with iris and ferns. Here, paths and steps are more formal, and benches provide places to rest and view the lake. Continuing along the west path, you find a cherry orchard with a traditional *Azumaya* or garden shelter. The moon-viewing stand on the water's edge is used in late summer for ceremonies celebrating the rising of the moon.

GARDEN OPEN: 10am–dusk

TOURS: Docent-led tours may be arranged upon request. Free *chado* demonstrations given on the third Saturday of the month, April–October, at 1:30pm

ADMISSION: $2.50 adults, $1.50 children, students, and seniors, children under 5 free

FURTHER INFORMATION FROM: Seattle Department of Parks and Recreation 100 Dexter Avenue North Seattle 98109-5199. 206.684.4725

From here, you may see koi and frogs among the water lilies, and perhaps a great blue heron. The tea garden or *roji*, meaning "dew-covered ground," is a sacred area of moss and dense plantings inspired by a mountain retreat. It is separated from the rest of the garden by a hedge of boxwood, cedar, and osmanthus. In the teahouse, students study *chado* (The Way of Tea), a 500-year old artistic discipline. The original teahouse, a gift from the people of Tokyo, was hand-constructed in Japan and reassembled on site. After it was destroyed by fire in 1973, the teahouse was rebuilt in 1981 with help from the Uransenke Foundation in Kyoto. That year, management of the garden was transferred from the University of Washington to the Seattle Department of Parks and Recreation. Further south is a waterfall and mountain stream with maidenhead ferns and an 11-tiered pagoda on the slope beyond it. An arching stone bridge transports visitors back to the entrance.

GARDEN OPEN: Dawn to dusk daily. Visitor center open from 9am–5pm daily, except Thanksgiving and Christmas Day
ADMISSION: Free
FURTHER INFORMATION FROM:
12001 Main Street
Bellevue 98005-3522.
425.452.2750
www.bellvuebotanical.org

ABOVE: *Japanese Garden with Kobe Friendship lantern*

23 Bellevue: Bellevue Botanical Garden

LOCATION: 10 MILES EAST OF SEATTLE, I-405 NE 8TH STREET EXIT

Located in a public park on a hill above downtown is a garden that is awe-inspiring for those of us who love the artfully designed chaos of a gloriously big perennial border. Opened to the public in 1992, the Bellevue Botanical Garden is a cooperative effort of the Bellevue Botanical Garden Society and the Bellevue Park and Community Services Department. The garden encompasses 36 acres of rolling hills, undisturbed woodland, meadows, bogs, a Japanese garden, a loop trail, and individual display gardens for fuchsias, groundcovers, and water-wise plants. Its most spectacular garden—one that draws garden lovers from afar—is the mixed perennial border, a massive undertaking that has achieved sumptuous results. The Northwest Perennial Alliance created and now maintains the perennial border. Its mission is to educate the public about old plant cultivars in danger of being lost or forgotten and new cultivars worthy of home gardens. The border is a tribute to thousands of hours of volunteer labor and hundreds of yards of steaming manure used to amend the heavy clay soil. Spanning

17,000 square-feet, it runs north to south just west of the visitor center, along a hillside site that is 300 feet long and 90 feet across at its widest. With a backbone of native shrubs and trees such as barberries, dogwoods, elders, and roses, the perennial border lends a uniquely Northwest twist to a garden feature popularized in England. The foliage and blooms create waves of color, including a hot border, one of pinks, whites, and variegated foliage, another of yellows, deep blues, and blacks, and a lovely mix of lavenders and apricots. Coming out of the woods into full sun at the south end of the hot border, visitors are amazed at the waves of crimson crocosmias, salmon day lilies, and gold St. John's wort swarming with hummingbirds, bees, and butterflies. The north end offers cooler colors in a double border of roses, peonies, coneflowers, catmint, and Russian sage. Though mid-summer is peak for the border, color and texture from interesting barks, berries, and foliage creates interest nearly year-round. The visitor center is in the former home of Calhoun and Harriet Short, who donated the house and seven acres to the city.

24 Wenatchee: Ohme Gardens

LOCATION: ABOUT 1/2 MILE NORTH OF WENATCHEE, NEAR JUNCTION OF
HIGHWAYS 2 AND 97A, 150 MILES EAST OF SEATTLE

High on a bluff overlooking the Wenatchee Valley, the Columbia River, and the Cascade Mountains looming in the west is a remarkable garden of evergreens and alpine meadows crafted over a period of 60 years by the Ohme family. In 1929, newlyweds Herman and Ruth Ohme moved to this site with panoramic views of the valley to start an orchard. Intending to build a quiet retreat, they began to create a small piece of the Cascade Mountains on two acres of the arid, rocky site that grew little but sagebrush. The Ohmes dug up thousands of small evergreens, shrubs, and wildflowers in the Cascades and carried them home in their Studebaker Coupe. Using an old army stretcher or a mule and plank sled, they hauled in hundreds of tons of flagstone and other rocks for pathways, pools, and borders. Hand watering their transplants with truckloads of five-gallon jugs, they transformed the landscape into a lush high-mountain garden with wildflower meadows, lawns, waterfalls, and shaded pools rimmed with ferns. They built a stone lookout point, dozens of stone benches, and rustic shelters from logs they cut in the mountains, with hand-peeled cedar bark for roofing and siding. In 1939, encouraged by delighted visitors,

GARDEN OPEN: 9am–6pm April 15–Memorial Day; 9am–7pm June–Labor Day; 9am–6pm Labor Day–October 15
ADMISSION: $6 adults, $3 ages 7-17, children under 6 free
FURTHER INFORMATION FROM: 3327 Ohme Road Wenatchee 98801. 509.662.5785 www.ohmegardens.com

Columbia River view from Ohme Gardens

the Ohmes opened their "backyard" to the public, charging 25 cents per carload. After Herman's death in 1971, Ruth continued to tend her creation until her own death at the age of 87 in 1997. Their son Gordon took over as head gardener in 1971 and expanded the garden from four acres to its present nine. In 1991, the Ohmes sold their now-public but still restful retreat to the state, which turned over management to Chelan County. Today, the combination of craggy rock outcroppings, water, and carpet-like swaths of creeping phlox and thyme, sedums, vinca, and mosses continue the Ohme's legacy of creating a natural mountain garden in the high desert of central Washington.

OPEN: 8am–1/2 hour before dusk

ADMISSION: Free

FURTHER INFORMATION FROM: Spokane Parks and Recreation Department West 4-21st Avenue Spokane 99203. 509.625.6622

The Renaissance-style annual garden

25 Spokane: Manito Park and Botanical Gardens

LOCATION: IN THE SOUTH PART OF SPOKANE, ON GRAND BOULEVARD BETWEEN 17TH AND 25TH AVENUES

In 1903, the city of Spokane changed the name of Montrose Park, an undeveloped recreation area, to Manito, meaning "spirit" or "spirit of nature" in the Algonquin Indian language. For some years, Manito Park's main attractions were its exhibition gardens and a small zoo. From 1907 to 1913, the city's Park Board oversaw development of the park's 90 acres, including recreational facilities, botanical gardens, and a conservatory for tropical plants. During this era, the park also constructed a three-acre, sunken, Renaissance-style garden designed by John W. Duncan with an elaborate central granite fountain and symmetrical beds of annual flowers. Since those early years, other gardens have been added, such as the Joel E. Ferris Perennial Garden, with English-style beds displaying 39,000 square feet of hundreds of plant species. This great collection of plants blooms from early spring with bulbs and primroses, through summer's lupines, delphiniums, and coneflowers, and into fall with chrysanthemums, heliopsis, and rudbeckia. In a sunny rock garden are mineral-loving plants such as pink phlox, white candytuft, and basket-of-gold alyssum that spill over a wall. The Spokane Rose Society joined the Parks Department in creating the six-acre Rose Hill, an old-fashioned rose garden displaying 1,700 rose bushes of 225 varieties. Rose Hill is an All-America Rose Selections display garden, and also a test site for the Dahlia Society of Spokane. A semicircular

arbor of 14 Tuscan columns encourages climbing roses. The
Nishinomiya Japanese Garden, named in honor of Spokane's
sister city, was designed by Nagao Sakurai and opened in 1974.
This traditional Japanese-style garden artfully combines landscape architecture with ornaments of rock, a contemplation
shelter, stone lanterns, and water features such as a pond and
waterfall. In late spring, the lilac garden offers fragrant clouds
of blossoms, many of them from bushes cultivated from slips
sent by Nishinomiya to honor the friendship between the two
cities. Elsewhere in the park, a duck pond, picnic areas, a café,
and playgrounds (one with a wading pool) keep children happy
when they aren't exploring the gardens.

26 Federal Way: Rhododendron Species Botanical Garden

LOCATION: ON WEYERHAEUSER COMPANY CAMPUS: I-5, EXIT 143, BETWEEN
TACOMA AND SEATTLE

GARDEN OPEN: 10am–4pm
March–May (closed
Thursday), 11am–4pm
June–February (closed
Thursday and Friday)
ADMISSION: $3.50, $2.50
seniors and students, chil-
dren under 12 free
FURTHER INFORMATION FROM:
PO Box 3798
Federal Way 98063.
253.838.4646
www.halcyon.com/rsf/
NEARBY SIGHTS OF INTEREST:
Pacific Rim Bonsai Collection

The 22-acre Rhododendron Species Botanical Garden is home
to one of the largest collections of species rhododendrons and
azaleas in the world. This well-labeled collection consists of
more than 10,000 rhododendrons representing 450 species—
half the world's total number—from the wilds of North
America, Europe, Asia, and Australia. The region's mild climate allows a long blooming season. From early January
through July, these wild beauties bloom in shades of pure
white to soft pink, clear yellow, Creamsicle orange, flame red,
and deep violet. The majority bloom from March through May;
the garden's last species to bloom is *Rhododendron
auriculatum*, a beautiful multi-trunked plant with large white
trumpet flowers that exude a citrus-like fragrance. One of the
garden's missions is to educate the public about the enormous
diversity of the genus. It ranges from prostrate groundcovers
from China that grow no more than a few inches to 100-foot-
tall trees from the lower Himalayan Mountains. Wild rhododendrons are found from sea level to 19,000 feet in elevation,
and in habitats from the tropics to alpine regions. Their leaves
may be one-quarter-inch long to over three feet. Some in the
collection, such as the *Rhododendron
macrophyllum* (or "rose tree with large
leaves"), the state flower of Washington,
are native to the region. The azaleas, also a
member of the rhododendron genus,
include both deciduous and the less common evergreen azaleas from Asia.
Complementing the rhododendrons and

Rhododendron auriculatum
blooms in mid-summer

azaleas in a woodland setting are companion plantings of ferns, primroses, iris, heathers, viburnums, magnolias, maples, conifers, and perennial flowers. At the center of the garden is a gazebo that overlooks much of the landscape. To re-create a Himalayan mountain slope, more than 200 tons of Cascade granite were hauled in for the alpine garden, which features tiny rhododendrons that thrive in harsh, windswept, colder conditions. A pond garden, a woodland area, and individual gardens devoted to heathers, ferns, and carnivorous companion plants complete the collection. The garden grows some of its collection for sale, including the Golden Comet azalea (*Rhododendron luteum*), with a very fragrant, bright yellow-orange flower and scarlet foliage in the fall. The garden is managed by the Rhododendron Species Foundation, a non-profit organization dedicated to research, conservation, and cultivation of wild rhododendrons. The foundation, founded in 1964, created the original garden at the home of Dr. Milton Walker of Eugene, Oregon. In 1974, the Weyerhaeuser Company offered the current site on its corporate campus, and the garden was moved and reopened in 1977.

GARDEN OPEN: 10am–4pm March through May (closed Thursday); 11am–4pm June through February (closed Thursday and Friday)

ADMISSION: Free

TOURS: Guided tours offered Sunday at noon

FURTHER INFORMATION FROM:
Bonsai Collection
Weyerhaeuser Company
33663 Weyerhaeuser Way South
Federal Way, 98003.
253.924.5206
www.weyerhaeuser.com/bonsai

NEARBY SIGHTS OF INTEREST:
Rhododendron Species Botanical Garden

27 Federal Way: Pacific Rim Bonsai Collection

LOCATION: ON WEYERHAEUSER COMPANY CAMPUS: I-5, EXIT 143, BETWEEN TACOMA AND SEATTLE

Located within the forest on the Weyerhaeuser corporate campus adjacent to the Rhododendron Species Botanical Garden, the Pacific Rim Bonsai Collection is a permanent outdoor gallery of living art. It includes more than 50 outstanding examples of bonsai art from the Pacific Rim nations of China, Japan, Korea, Taiwan, Canada, and the United States. In 1989, the Weyerhaeuser Company created the collection in honor of its trade relations with Pacific Rim nations and as a tribute to the Washington State Centennial. Bonsai (pronounced "bone-sigh") is a Japanese word that means "a tree in a pot." This art of pruning trees to create miniature versions was first depicted in second-century writings of the Chinese, who called it *penzai*. Bonsai later flourished in Japan and developed into the art form as we know it today. Displayed outside against beige stucco walls, the collection includes a tiny grove of Japanese maples, a crabapple tree, and a firethorn, whose twisted, exposed roots and thin, distinctly layered branches illustrate the Chinese bonsai style called "dragon claws."

28 Orting: The Chase Garden

LOCATION: IN ORTING, ABOUT 1.5 HOURS OR 50+ MILES SOUTH OF SEATTLE

In 1959, after Emmott and Ione Chase built their home on a bluff overlooking the Puyallup River, they hired landscape architect Rex Zumwalt to design a garden to take advantage of their rural setting and a spectacular view of Mount Rainier. Zumwalt planned the gardens immediately around the Japanese-style house, which was oriented toward the outdoors with numerous decks, a large patio, two free-form pools, and a quirky outdoor dance floor. When the Chases began their garden, they knew little about landscaping and had little to invest in their garden. But in the decades since, they have created a splendid example of Northwest-style garden design with natural contours, native plants, and a distinctly Japanese influence. Their four-and-a-half-acre garden includes open meadow, a woodland garden, and a stroll garden that Ione modestly describes as "a small effort at rock gardening." Since 1995, the Chases, well on in years, have worked with the Garden Conservancy to preserve and maintain the property, with the help of a local volunteer group, the Friends of the Chase Garden. The most colorful time for the garden is in the spring, when trilliums and other native flowers bloom in the forest garden. Emerging from the forest onto a sunny slope dominated by a huge hemlock, the garden unfolds below and around you. A great lawn extends to the edge of a cliff with the view of Mount Rainier beyond. On the slope, pea-gravel paths lead to tapestries of rock plants such as phlox, gentians, primulas, lithodora, and double arabis. Two small bridges cross a dry streambed where groundcovers grow in profusion. The garden's use of rocks, gravel, driftwood, and restrained use of plants creates a sense of great serenity.

GARDEN OPEN: By appointment from mid-April to mid-May
ADMISSION: $3 includes guided tour
FURTHER INFORMATION FROM:
Rosina McIvor
c/o The Chase Garden
P.O. Box 98553
Des Moines 98198.
206.242.4040

A reflecting pool flanked by alpine fir trees

GARDEN OPEN: 10am–4:30pm
daily, closed Thanksgiving
and Christmas Day

ADMISSION: Free (donations
appreciated)

FURTHER INFORMATION FROM:
316 South G Street
Tacoma 98405.
253.591.5330
www.takomaparks.com

NEARBY SIGHTS OF INTEREST:
Port Defiance Park

29 Tacoma: W.W. Seymour Botanical Conservatory

LOCATION: WITHIN TACOMA'S WRIGHT PARK, ON SOUTH G STREET

The W.W. Seymour Botanical Conservatory is a Victorian jewel box perched on the edge of Wright Park in the historic Stadium district of Tacoma. It is special for several reasons: It is one of only three Victorian-style conservatories on the West Coast; it is listed on the National Register of Historic Places; and it is simply a beautiful and remarkable structure with an interesting collection of more than 200 species of tropical plants. Built in 1908 with funds contributed by William W. Seymour, a utilities, lumber, and land baron (and later mayor of Tacoma), the conservatory was rebuilt in 1937 by the Works Progress Administration, and restored again in 1956, 1976, and 1992. The 12-sided central dome—a relatively small 40 feet across and 45 feet tall—is composed of more than 4,000 panes of glass with copper panels. The conservatory's 3,600 square feet, including the entrance wing and two other small display wings, feel intimate, more like a conservatory for a private estate than for a public garden. The air is warm and moist and filled with

Palms, cycads, fuchsias, and orchids fill the W.W. Seymour Botanical Conservatory.

water music from a waterfall and small koi pond. We can imagine a Victorian-era plant collector happily picking fruit from the lemon and grapefruit trees and tending to the colorful displays of annuals such as pink begonias and golden celosias that are changed monthly. The plant collection evokes the era's passion for exotic plants, such as lilies, bromeliads, bird of paradise, and a Queen Sago palm. Other unusual plants include numerous epiphytes, or plants that live on the surface of other plants, such as orchids, ferns, and tiny epiphytic rhododendrons. In the tropical room, creeping fig adorns walls built of lava-like rock—a byproduct of copper production from a since-closed local foundry. Part of the conservatory's mission is to increase environmental stewardship by displaying plants in different environments that are managed biologically, without chemicals, a change in recent years that has lead to healthier, more vigorous plants, according to conservatory staff. Owned and operated by the Metropolitan Park District of Tacoma, the conservatory releases approximately 500,000 beneficial bugs each year to control garden pests—though it's unlikely you'll ever see one amidst the lush foliage and blooms.

30 Tacoma: Point Defiance Park

LOCATION: IN NORTHWEST TACOMA, AT 5400 NORTH PEARL STREET, AT THE
END OF POINT DEFIANCE PENINSULA

GARDEN OPEN: Dawn to dusk daily

ADMISSION: Free

FURTHER INFORMATION FROM:
Metroparks/North Division
Maintenance
4702 South 19th Street
Tacoma 98405.
253.305.1000
www.tacomaparks.com

NEARBY SIGHTS OF INTEREST:
W.W. Seymour Botanical
Conservatory

Even in the rain, the gardens at Point Defiance Park are sure to lift your spirits. I strolled through early one cool, drizzly July morning and found such an abundance of color and fragrance that I found it hard to leave. Laid out toward the point at the end of the park, a peninsula that extends into Puget Sound, the gardens present an exuberant medley of saturated colors— reds, yellows, pinks, corals, purples, greens—that seem all the richer against the gray mist. There are seven different gardens devoted to roses, fuchsias, iris, dahlias, herbs, Northwest natives, and the traditional garden style of Japan. The All-American Rose Selections display garden shows off some 1,500 rose bushes. The beds are arranged in a circle around a gazebo, winding like ribbons in gorgeous hues, from the delicate mauve of Lagerfeld to the deep-rose H.G. Anderson to the palest-yellow, cabbage-like blooms of Elina. Next to the roses, the dahlia test garden offers hundreds of new cultivars for inspection before introduction to the market. Some of them look like they belong in the gardens of giants, especially Gay Triumph with spiky-looking, peach-colored flowers the size of dinner plates. A "tunnel" of climbing roses leads to three long pergola-covered promenades of annuals and perennials—lilies in hues of lemon, peach, and nectarine, blue and pink

A classic rose garden surrounding the gazebo

hydrangeas, and Victorian-era annuals such as begonias and dusty miller. The fuchsias—scarlet and purple blooms hanging from tiny and massive shrubs—are arranged in parterre beds with arborvitae hedges. At the end of the point overlooking the Sound is the Japanese garden and its focal point, the tile-roofed pagoda, a replica of a seventeenth-century Japanese lodge. Built in 1914 as a streetcar terminus, it was dedicated as a garden center in 1963. A cinnabar-colored arched footbridge, stone lanterns, and bamboo fences detail this tranquil garden with a waterfall, stream, and nooks with benches that offer quiet spots for meditation or observation. In 1868, President Andrew Johnson originally set aside the 698-acre park, one of the 20 largest urban parks in the country, as a military reservation. In 1888, President Grover Cleveland approved a bill that allowed Tacoma to use the reserve as a public park, and in 1905, the City of Tacoma obtained control of the park. Renowned landscape architect S.R. Hare of Kansas City, Missouri, designed a comprehensive plan for the park in 1911 that included athletic facilities, a zoological garden, a "forest primeval," and miles of paths and trails. Today, the gravel paths in the gardens are generally wheelchair accessible. The park's remaining acreage spans lawns, wooded areas, and a couple of abandoned garden areas with their own mystique. At the east end of the park is a zoo and aquarium where, for a fee, you can also enjoy a camellia garden.

GARDEN OPEN: 10am–4pm Thursday, Saturday, Sunday, Monday, and 12pm–8pm, Friday, April–September; 10am–3pm Friday–Sunday, October–March

ADMISSION: $5, $3 senior, student, and military, children under 12 free.

FURTHER INFORMATION FROM: 12317 Gravelly Lake Drive SW Lakewood 98499. 253.584.4106 or toll free: 888.858.4106 www.lakewold.org

31 Lakewood: Lakewold Gardens

LOCATION: ON THE WEST SIDE OF GRAVELLY LAKE, EXIT 124 ON I-5, JUST SOUTH OF TACOMA

Lakewold Gardens' ten acres of rolling lawns, topiary, and formal and woodland gardens represent some of the most elegant and serene elements of garden design. The gardens' history as a placid retreat on Gravelly Lake goes back nearly a century to Emma Alexander, who had a cabin here in 1908. Her son, H.F. Alexander, and his wife Ruth had their home and gardens designed to capture views of the lake. The Alexanders were influenced by the renowned Olmsted Brothers of Brookline, Massachusetts, in the design of the perimeter wall, gate, and a 230-foot herringbone brick walkway leading from the house to the teahouse that they had built for their daughter's wedding in 1922. The Alexanders sold the property in 1925 to the Griggs family, who named it Lakewold, Middle English for "lakewoods." Corydon and Eulalie Wagner bought Lakewold in 1938 and began five decades of planting, shaping, and shearing the garden. This was done mostly under the guidance of Thomas Church, one of America's finest landscape architects, who came to Lakewold on his first visit to the Pacific Northwest in 1958 and returned regularly to suggest refinements to the garden design. Eulalie, who had become an accomplished plant collector, continued to garden after her husband's death in 1978, and in 1987 donated the entire estate to a nonprofit organization, Friends of Lakewold. From the Wagner's Georgian-style home, the brick walk provides a grand promenade past topiary shaped as waterfowl and boxwood-edged parterre beds. To the right, on the edge of the great lawn, is the "wolf tree," a giant Douglas fir hundreds of years old that shelters ferns and Japanese maples in a woodland garden. To the left is Church's beautifully balanced design of a sundial, lion fountain, and quatrefoil (four-leafed) pool on axis with Mount Rainier. Now transformed into a water garden, the pool satisfied both Corydon's desire for a swimming pool and Eulalie's for a decorative one. The wooden teahouse, rebuilt in 1992, is embellished with a Chinese reflecting bowl, statuary, and large pots with such unusual plants as fragrant, melon-colored Charles Grimaldi angel trumpets. A gravel path leads to a lookout above a natural garden with an alpine stream. This area was selected by Gardens for Peace as a symbol of reflection and meditation. The path continues past three waterfalls planted with bulbs, orchids, rhododendrons, and azaleas; the lowest area includes bog plants and primroses. From the lake, a path leads through a wooded area past rare Himalayan blue poppies, which bloom for about a month beginning in mid-May, to a rock garden with dianthus, heathers, and Asian lilies. A woodland path leads to a rose garden behind the house where roses flourish in the warm colors of coral, yellow and red that Eulalie loved. Nearby, santolina and germander create a knot garden, while pottage and culinary herbs stand ready for the kitchen.

Topiary birds perched amid boxwood-edged parterres

ALASKA

YUKON

NOME

17 FAIRBANKS

DENALI NAT'L PARK

PALMER

ANCHORAGE
15

16

JUNEAU

1

KAUAI HAENA
LAWAI LIHUE

NIHAU

2,3

10

WAHIAWA

11

HALEIWA

OAHU

KANEOHE

HONOLULU
6-9

KOKO

5

MOLAKAI

HAWAII

LANAI

MAUI

HANA

12,13

KAHOOLAWW

PAPAIKOU

14

HILO

HAWAII

1 Kauai: Limahuli Garden and Preserve

2 Kauai: Lawai Garden

3 Kauai: Allerton Garden

4 Oahu: Ho`omaluhia Botanical Garden

5 Oahu: Koko Crater Botanical Garden

6 Oahu: Harold L. Lyon Arboretum

7 Oahu: Queen Emma Summer Palace and

Garden

8 Oahu: Foster Botanical Garden

9 Oahu: Lili`uokalani Botanical Garden

10 Oahu: Wahiawa Botanic Garden

11 Oahu: Waimea Arboretum and Botanical

Gardens

12 Maui: Kahanu Garden

13 Maui: Kula Botanical Garden

14 Hawaii: Hawaii Tropical Botanical Garden

15 Anchorage: Alaska Botanical Garden

16 Palmer: Matanuska Valley Agricultural

Showcase Garden

17 Fairbanks: The Georgeson Botanical Garden

Noncontinental United States

Hawaii and Alaska

Set among some of the world's most spectacular scenery, the public gardens of Alaska and Hawaii couldn't be more diverse in their plant material, climate, and growing conditions. Alaska's intense, condensed growing season and extreme ranges in temperature and sunlight are the virtual opposite of Hawaii's year-round tropical gardens, which experience more moderate temperatures and steadier amounts of sunlight. They have in common, however, a certain lushness and intensity that sets them apart from gardens on the mainland. And given the borrowed scenery of many Alaskan and Hawaiian gardens, they can be quite spectacular.

Hawaii's public gardens, located on four of the archipelago's eight major islands, exemplify the garden world's notions of the wild, sultry, and exotic—waterfalls, colorful and unusual plants such as bromeliads and orchids, and breathtaking views of the Pacific Ocean. Tropical plants thrive on year-round temperatures that rarely dip below 60 degrees and more often are in the 70s and 80s, with frequent showers. The islands vary, however, from arid zones in extinct volcanoes such as Koko Crater on Oahu, to green, leafy, and jungle-like gardens that reach from the valley floor high into the rainforest, as on Kauai, "the garden island."

From the days when the shipping trade thrived in the mid-1800s, Hawaii has been a repository for botanical specimens from around the world, especially Asia and the Pacific Islands. Foster Botanical Garden on Oahu got its start during this period of plant exploration and importation. As in Alaska, some of Hawaii's gardens evolved in the last century from agricultural lands such as sugar plantations that were transformed by horticulturists from the mainland. Two historic gardens—Queen Emma's Summer Palace on Oahu and Allerton Garden on Kauai—were begun more than a century ago by a gifted royal gardener, Queen Emma, the widow of King Kamehameha IV. Several, including Limahuli Garden and Preserve on Kauai and Kahanu Garden on Hawaii, are steeped in the cultural history of the Hawaiian and Polynesian people and preserve ancient architectural and spiritual sites. The Lawai Garden on Kauai, headquarters for the National Tropical Botanical Garden, which owns and manages four Hawaiian gardens, and the Honolulu Botanical Garden on Oahu, which oversees five gardens, are using conservation, research, and education to protect the legacy of native Hawaiian plants.

Given the challenge of long winters, with short days, nine months of snow, and temperatures dipping to below zero, Alaska's gardens are dormant much of the year. But come summer, the plants grow rapidly, given long days of intense sunlight. Around the summer solstice in June, Alaskans celebrate nearly round-the-clock sunlight, which encourages plants to grow almost before your eyes; three-foot-tall petunias and 50-pound cabbages are some of the amazing results. The relatively cool temperatures—often in the mid-60s in summer—encourage brilliant colors in the flowers. And Alaskans do love their flowers: The city of Anchorage plants 520 flower beds at 72 parks and public places, and is decked out with 100,000 hanging baskets during the summer months. Statewide, the best public gardens include The Georgeson Botanical Garden in Fairbanks, which began as an agricultural station for homesteaders a century ago, and the Alaska Botanical Garden in Anchorage, devoted to hardy native and introduced plants, which was established less than a decade ago.

Kauai: Limahuli Garden and Preserve

LOCATION: ON KAUAI'S NORTH SHORE, AT THE END OF KUHIO HIGHWAY IN HAENA

Surrounded by mountains with peaks as sharp as shark's teeth, the Limahuli Valley on Kauai's northern Na Pali coast is one of the "garden island's" sacred sites, sheltering rare plants, archeological ruins, and vivid lore passed down from the first Hawaiians. Sheltered within this wet and wild valley is an extraordinary rain forest garden with lofty views of the Pacific Ocean. Located *mauka* (on the mountain side) of the coast road, Limahuli Garden is part of the National Tropical Botanical Garden(NTBG), a Congressionally chartered institution for research, conservation, and education on tropical plants. Some of the first Polynesians settled near Limahuli, which means "turning hands." The garden contains a series of stone terraces used to grow taro that were built 700 to 1,000 years ago, as well as ruins of ancient houses and what it is believed to be a religious site. Juliet Rice Wichman (whose missionary family has owned the valley since the 1940s) laid out the garden in the 1960s, and in 1976 gave it to the NTBG as a place to preserve and cultivate native plants. The garden's director is her grandson, horticulturist Charles "Chipper" Wichman, who has worked at Limahuli for 25 years. Open to the public since 1995, the garden focuses on collections of rare and endangered plants native to Hawaii, plants of ethnobotanical value, and the preservation of natural ecosystems such as the Limahuli Stream, one

GARDEN OPEN: 9:30–4pm Tuesday–Friday and Sunday
ADMISSION: $15 for 2-hour guided tour (reservations required); $10 for self-guided tour
FURTHER INFORMATION FROM:
Limahuli Garden
Box 808
Hanalei, Kauai 96714.
808.826.1053
www.ntbg.org

Taro terraces with day lilies in foreground at Limahuli Garden and Preserve

*Taro terraces are cradled in a
cirque of sacred peaks.*

of the islands' few remaining pristine streams. Adjacent to the
garden is the 985-acre Limahuli Preserve, which Chipper
Wichman gave to the NTBG in 1994. The preserve, which is
closed to the public, protects about 100 native plants representing 70 percent of Kauai's—and more than half of the state's—
endangered species. Some of them are propagated and on view
in the public garden, such as *Pisonia wagneriana*, a member of
the four o'clock family with sticky seeds that the early
Hawaiians used to catch birds whose bright feathers were
woven into capes and headdresses. In contrast to some of
Hawaii's showier ornamental gardens, this garden honors the
natural setting and its many shades and textures of green. One
of the few splashes of vibrant color—an embankment of tangerine day lilies—greets you near the entrance. The half-mile
trail through the garden begins on a lawn surrounded by breadfruit and candlenut trees. Ahead, the Limahuli Stream trickles
through the taro terraces. The roots of these small, water-loving
plants are used to make poi, the fermented paste that was the
ancient Hawaiians' most important food (eight varieties grow
here; the ancients, by contrast, grew more than 300). The path
winds up the hillside through the rain forest, past mountain
apple, screwpine, and shampoo ginger with red flower heads

and aromatic sap. Further along the trail are yellow strawberry guava and frangipani, whose fragrant flowers are used in leis. The garden's highest point offers panoramic views of the valley and terraces below, as well as of the coral reefs and cobalt waters of the Pacific. Towering above is a great cirque of jagged peaks, including *Makana*, or "gift," the mountain referred to as Bali Hai in *South Pacific*. The sacred spirit of the mountains lives in lore and is almost palpable in this garden.

2 Kauai: Lawai Garden

LOCATION: IN THE LAWAI VALLEY, NEAR POIPU ON KAUAI'S SOUTH SHORE

On the slopes of the picturesque Lawai Valley is the Lawai Garden, headquarters of the National Tropical Botanical Garden. The NTBG is a privately funded, nonprofit organization, comprising four gardens and three preserves in Hawaii and a fifth garden in Florida. More than two-thirds of the earth's known plant species grow in the tropics, and many of them are disappearing faster than they can be collected or studied. NTBG has assembled the world's largest collection of federally-listed endangered plant species, including the largest collection of native Hawaiian flora. NTBG scientists have discovered more than 30 new species during plant exploration trips through the Pacific Islands, and sometimes embark on harrowing rescue missions, such as rappelling off cliffs to hand-pollinate endangered plants. The first site to be acquired by NTBG in the late 1960s, Lawai Garden spans 259 acres of garden and preserve. Opened in 1971 on former sugar cane fields, it is home to NTBG's main nursery, herbarium, and research library. Though it is not a classic display or estate garden (the NTBG's adjacent Allerton Garden fulfills that role), the Lawai Garden presents exquisite, colorful, and noteworthy plants—such as a collection of brilliant coral trees (*Erithrina*). The two-and-a-half-hour tour offers a veritable Noah's Ark of tropical flora, with significant collections of palms, flowering trees, heliconias, and orchids. The setting is so exotic and dramatic, in fact, that a dozen films have been shot here, including *Jurassic Park*. Tours begin at the visitor center, a restored 1920s sugar plantation cottage located next to the Lawai Garden on a scenic knoll across from the famed Spouting Horn blowhole in Poipu. The gardens around the cottage recall the plantation era. From here a fleet of vintage open jitneys transports visitors over dirt roads to begin the walking tours of Lawai and Allerton Garden.

GARDEN OPEN: Two-and-a-half-hour guided tours scheduled at 9am and 2pm on Mondays, by reservation
ADMISSION: $25
FURTHER INFORMATION FROM:
National Tropical Botanical Garden
P.O. Box 340
Lawai, Kauai 96765.
808.742.2623
www.ntbg.org

Plantation cottage beside the perennial garden

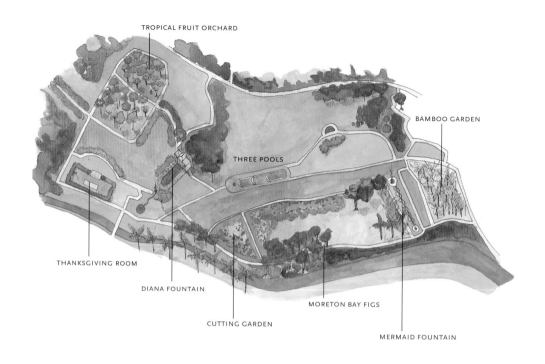

TROPICAL FRUIT ORCHARD

BAMBOO GARDEN

THREE POOLS

THANKSGIVING ROOM

DIANA FOUNTAIN

CUTTING GARDEN

MORETON BAY FIGS

MERMAID FOUNTAIN

3 Kauai: Allerton Garden

LOCATION: BETWEEN LAWAI GARDEN AND LAWAI BAY, ON KAUAI'S SOUTH SHORE

Beside the stream that flows through the lush Lawai Valley to the ocean at Lawai-Kai is the historic Allerton Garden, which is characterized by an elegant blend of European art and design and the exotic flowers and trees of the tropics. Set amidst pathways, fountains, pools, and sculptures, the Allerton Garden seems steeped in a quiet and profound grace in which classical garden architecture meets nature in a dreamy, timeless way. The 100-acre garden is owned by the Allerton Gardens Trust and managed by the National Tropical Botanical Garden (NTBG), whose headquarters are located at the adjacent Lawai Garden.

Successive caretakers of this landscape have preserved its natural beauty and remnants of its rich history. The ancient Polynesians built fishponds and cultivated taro, a staple of their diet, along the Lawai Stream. Queen Emma, the widow of King Kamehameha IV, began the gardens at Lawai-kai. In 1870-71, she resided here in a large frame house with a thatch roof on the bluff above the beach. She planted lovely fuchsia and white spider lilies that bear her name and the luxurious magenta bougainvillea that spills over the cliffs. Her letters from Lawai requested plant slips of Lauae ferns, rose apple, mango, and pandanus, all of which still grow in the valley. Queen Emma was deeded the land in 1871, the year she left Lawai never to return. Five years later, she leased the land to plantation developer Duncan McBryde, whose family ten years later planted the upper valley with sugar cane and let the lower valley to Chinese rice growers and taro farmers. In 1899, his son, Alexander McBryde, a founder of the McBryde Sugar Company, was granted a parcel of the garden in the lower portion of the Lawai Valley. He continued to develop the valley botanically, planting palms, gingers, plumerias, and ferns in cooperation with a Dr. Wilder, an early plant collector on Kauai. McBryde had Queen Emma's cottage moved from the cliff to the valley floor around 1916, and lived in it for some years afterward.

The design of the garden was the work of Robert Allerton, a wealthy Illinois businessman, and his adopted son, John Gregg, who bought the property in 1938. Allerton studied painting, architecture, and landscape architecture in Europe, and had designed a series of formal gardens at his family's estate in Illinois. John Gregg, an architect, designed a house for the beachfront, while Allerton began designing and laying out the gardens. They created the garden using a broad palette— focusing on forms, textures, shapes, and foliage—as well as a sense of surprise, incorporating plants from collecting trips to Ceylon and the Caribbean. The line of the Lawai Stream

GARDEN OPEN: Two-and-a-half-hour tours at 9am, 10am, 1pm, 2pm, Tuesday through Saturday, by reservation
ADMISSION: $25
FURTHER INFORMATION FROM: Allerton Garden
P.O. Box 340
Lawai, Kauai 96765.
808.742.2623
www.ntbg.org

OPPOSITE: *The goddess of the woods, reflected in the pool in Diana's Garden*

Waterfalls and runnels create water music throughout the garden.

became the spine of the garden, with a series of garden rooms between the riverbank and cliffs that rise behind.

In his later years, Allerton petitioned Congress to establish the NTBG, and donated funds to purchase the land on which the Lawai Garden was established. After Robert's death at age 91 in 1964, John Gregg Allerton became a trustee of the estate. He also became an NTBG trustee and, as its first volunteer, began landscaping the Lawai Garden. After Hurricane Iniki blasted across Kauai in 1992, destroying hundreds of the Allerton and Lawai gardens' trees and shrubs, the gardens were closed for a couple of years for a renovation that involved replacing and moving plants and restoring many of the Allerton Garden's architectural features to recapture its spirit.

A tour of the Allerton Garden begins at the visitor center across from the Spouting Horn blowhole in Poipu. Vintage open jitneys transport you through the gates of the once-private estate, winding along a cliff road with enticing views of Lawai Bay. Below, the Allerton home gazes out to the sea, surrounded by coconut palms and a smooth green lawn that extends to a crescent-shaped beach.

Threatened green sea turtles nest on the protected beach, and humpback whales and monk seals swim offshore. The endangered Hawaiian gallinule and other native birds such as the Koloa duck and black-crowned night heron find sanctuary in the calm of the Lawai Stream.

A jungle-like path along the stream leads to a three-quarter-mile loop through a series of distinct garden "rooms" with artfully layered colors and textures. A canopy of monkeypod, banyan, and Longon trees forms a ceiling over many of the rooms and corridors. Gravity-fed fountains, pools, waterfalls, cascades, and runnels make water music throughout the gardens. Native stonework staircases, patios, and borders create a sense of unity that connects the separate spaces. Ocean breezes sweep gently through the Bamboo Garden, rustling the parchment-like leaves. Next to it, two whimsical bronze mermaids flank a 126-foot, zigzag, art deco channel through which water pulses like waves. Further upstream, massive Moreton Bay figs with huge buttress roots create a prehistoric feeling on the riverbank. The cutting garden expresses the Allertons' love for collecting plants such as orchids that are valued for their beauty and fragrance. The Thanksgiving Garden, with a reflecting pool and Italian bronze statues, commemorates where the Allertons once hosted a memorable Thanksgiving feast. Red-clawed heliconias hang above the path near a statue of Confucius.

Beyond is the NTBG nursery, where rare and endangered native Hawaiian plants are propagated. Before turning back toward the beach on the loop trail, visit the tropical fruit orchard, a Victory Garden during World War II, which contains trees such as mango, lychee, pomegranate, and star fruit. The Diana Fountain, where the goddess stands atop her pedestal gazing over a reflecting pool toward a loggia, is one of the most evocative places in the garden. Clutching her cloak, the moss-covered Roman goddess of woods and mountains, women and childbirth, surveys the solitary and tranquil scene. Further on, a lawn and dense foliage of giant elephant ear and birds' nest anthurium surround a dark cascade of three concrete pools embellished with scallop shells. Along the way are groves of pink and gold heliconias, masses of flowering gingers, and hillsides of frangipani. Upon leaving this tropical paradise, you'll once again ride through a gap where rock walls, shorn a century ago to accommodate sugar cane trains, now are adorned with maidenhair ferns.

A Chinese lantern decorates a quiet rocky spot at Allerton

GARDEN OPEN: 9am–4pm daily, closed New Year's Day and Christmas Day

ADMISSION: Free

GUIDED NATURE HIKES: 10am Saturday and 1pm Sunday

FURTHER INFORMATION FROM: 45-680 Luluku Road Kaneohe, Oahu 96744. 808.233.7323

4 Oahu: Ho`omaluhia Botanical Garden

LOCATION: IN KANEOHE, ON EASTERN SIDE OF OAHU, AT THE END OF LULUKU ROAD

*Ho`omaluhia* means, "to make a place of peace and tranquility," and this 400-acre botanical garden is designed for visitors to appreciate a natural state of grace. A wild and beautiful place, Ho`omaluhia is not a conventional botanic garden, but rather a natural park with interesting collections of plants, some of which are extinct in the wild. The garden is embraced by old crater walls that form a line of deeply textured *pali,* or cliffs, that spill over with waterfalls when it rains. Opened in 1982, Ho`omaluhia Botanical Garden was built as part of a dam project by the U.S. Army Corps of Engineers to provide flood protection for Kaneohe. It is one of five Honolulu Botanical Gardens owned and managed by the city and county of Honolulu. The botanical collection is composed mostly of trees and shrubs native to Hawaii and from major tropical regions worldwide. Collections with unusual specimens include palms, aroids, and heliconias. The collections are laid out geographically by region, including the Philippines, Sri Lanka and India, Malaysia, Africa, and tropical America. A road and a ten-mile network of trails connect these various garden areas with other facilities, including the 32-acre Waimaluhia ("peaceful waters") Lake, campgrounds, a day-use area, and a visitor center with an exhibit hall and botanical library.

A young Acacia Koa tree

5 Oahu: Koko Crater Botanical Garden

LOCATION: INSIDE KOKO CRATER, ON EASTERN SIDE OF OAHU, OFF KALANA-
IANAOLE HIGHWAY NEAR SANDY BEACH

Koko Crater, the landmark volcanic site near Hanauma Bay, contains one of the five Honolulu Botanical Gardens. Within this hot, dry, 200-acre site on the slopes and basin of a double crater is a garden that showcases xeriphytic, or drought-toler-ant, plants. Just past the Koko Crater Stables, colorful plumeria cultivars and bougainvillea greet visitors at the edge of the crater. Drinking water and hiking boots or sturdy shoes are a good idea if you wish to walk the dusty trail that leads to the inner crater floor. The trail passes through a thick growth of dryland plants such as *kiawe* and a grove of native green, orange-lipped, and orange-flowering *wiliwili* (*Erythrina sand-wicensis*). The one-and-a-half-hour self-guided walk leads visi-tors through plant collections of cacti, aloes, alluaudias, euphorbias, sansevierias, palms, and adeniums—arranged according to geographical place of origin, from America to Madagascar to Africa. Appropriated as a botanical garden in 1958, Koko Crater still is being planted, and offers no paved trails or facilities. Long-range plans include creating a xeriscape garden that will harmonize with the crater's environment and provide a model for conserving Oahu's precious water resources.

GARDEN OPEN: 9am–4pm, closed New Year's Day and Christmas Day
ADMISSION: Free
Guided tours by appointment
FURTHER INFORMATION FROM: Honolulu Botanical Gardens Department of Parks and Recreation
50 N. Vineyard Boulevard Honolulu, Oahu 96817.
808.522.7060

ABOVE: *Plumeria at Koko Crater Botanical Garden*

GARDEN OPEN: 9am–3pm
Monday through Saturday;
closed Sundays and Hawaiian
state holidays
ADMISSION: $1 (donation)
FURTHER INFORMATION FROM:
Lyon Arboretum
University of Hawaii at
Manoa
3860 Manoa Road
Honolulu, Oahu 96822.
808.988.0456
www.hawaii.edu/lyonarboretum

6 Oahu: Harold L. Lyon Arboretum

LOCATION: ON SOUTHEAST SIDE OF OAHU, OFF FREEWAY H-1, ON MANOA ROAD

Nestled against the Ko`olau Mountains, the Harold L. Lyon Arboretum offers spectacular panoramic views and the constant cloudy-then-sunny changes of fast-moving mountain and island weather. Be prepared: as a rain forest garden, it's often wet. A short walk uphill on the arboretum's main path leads to Inspiration Point and breathtaking views of undeveloped and protected land within the Manoa Valley. A bird watcher's paradise, the arboretum is home to zebra doves, red-whiskered bulbils, white-rumped shama, common mynahs, and the native Hawaiian 'Amakihi. About seven-and-a-half miles of trails wind through nearly half of the arboretum's 194 acres, planted with a rich assortment of about 5,000 native Hawaiian and exotic tropical plant species. Several generations ago, this landscape was barren, denuded by cattle grazing. The arboretum was founded in 1918 as a forest reconstruction project by the Hawaiian Sugar Planters' Association Experiment Station. The association acquired 124 acres and hired Harold L. Lyon, a young botanist from Minnesota, who planted about 2,000 tree species in what was then called the Manoa Arboretum. In 1953, Dr. Lyon persuaded the association to deed the arboretum to the University of Hawaii. When he died in 1957, the university named the arboretum and botanical garden for him. The university shifted the garden's focus from forestry to horticulture, and in recent years has dedicated itself to becoming a center for the rescue and propagation of rare and endangered native Hawaiian plants. In the Beatrice H. Krauss Ethnobotanical Garden, named after a botanist who encouraged the development of Hawaiian ethnobotany (the study of the plant lore of a people or race), you'll find various plants once used by ancient Hawaiians, introduced by the Polynesians after their voyages across the Pacific. The garden design includes about 40 species of plants grouped according to their natural habitat associations or uses as food, clothing, construction materials, medicine, dyes or musical instruments. In the north part of this garden are terraces featuring *kalo* (Hawaiian for taro), an important food plant, and elsewhere you'll find *kukui* (candlenuts), `*Ohe* (bamboo), *Ko* (sugar cane), and *awa* (kava). The arboretum also features areas devoted to herbs and spice plants, a Chinese-style garden, and two memorial gardens. Among the arboretum's collection of gorgeous tropical plants are gingers, heliconias, and one of the largest collections of palms, with more than 600 varieties.

Bromeliad garden in Fern Valley

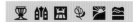

7 Oahu: Queen Emma Summer Palace and Garden

LOCATION: ON PALI HIGHWAY, NEAR DOWNTOWN HONOLULU

GARDEN OPEN: 9am–4pm daily, except holidays
ADMISSION: Free ($5 for admission to house museum)
FURTHER INFORMATION FROM: Daughters of Hawaii
2913 Pali Highway
Honolulu, Oahu 96817.
808.595.6291

Located in the Nuuanu Valley, the Queen Emma Summer Palace was the country retreat of Queen Emma Na'ea, wife of Kamehameha IV, king of the Hawaiian Islands from 1854 to 1863. In 1856, a year after she married, Queen Emma inherited 65 acres on which stood a Greek Revival clapboard house that had been prefabricated in Boston and shipped in pieces around the Horn. In Queen Emma's day, the Palace was called *Hanaiakamalama* ("foster child of the light") after a Hawaiian demi-goddess, and was used as a retreat for the royal family during hot weather. Queen Emma was an avid gardener and kept a nursery on Queen Street in Honolulu. After she died in 1885 at the age of 49, the Hawaiian Monarchial Government purchased the estate. In 1911, the territorial government set aside the land as Nuuanu Park. The Daughters of Hawaii, a nonprofit preservation group, saved the house in 1913 when the construction of a baseball field threatened it with demolition. The Daughters operate the House, now a National Historic Site, as a museum of nineteenth-century Hawaiian history (on display are many of the royal couple's furnishings, including the ornate crib of their only child, Prince Albert Edward, who died at the age of four). Six white Doric columns support the roof of the front *lanai*, or porch. Across the front are tall Hawaiian ferns and candlenuts, Hawaii's state tree. The original garden was designed by Danish landscape architect H. Augustus Holstein, and in the Queen's time featured a water lily pond with a bridge to an island where she served tea. Today, a simpler garden greets visitors. A slate terrace with Victorian-era wrought-iron furniture invites visitors to enjoy views of roses, hibiscus, and lawns that extend over two acres of the site. The gardens also display lovely white and fuchsia spider lilies named for the Queen. Exotic trees such as royal palms, mangos, tamarinds, jack fruit, red-flowering octopus, and monkeypod rain trees (whose seed provides *lei* flowers) provide shady spots for resting and contemplating the life of the royal family in the Victorian era.

Queen Emma's Summer Palace

GARDEN OPEN: 9am–4pm
daily, closed on New Year's
Day and Christmas Day
ADMISSION: $5
FURTHER INFORMATION FROM:
Department of Parks and
Recreation
50 North Vineyard Boulevard
Honolulu, Oahu 96817.
808.522.7066

8   Oahu: Foster Botanical Garden

LOCATION: IN DOWNTOWN HONOLULU, ON VINEYARD BOULEVARD

The Foster Botanical Garden, Hawaii's oldest botanic garden,
offers a glimpse of Victorian times, when plant explorations and
exotic, even whimsical, tropical plants with economic potential
were all the rage. A young German doctor and botanist, Dr.
William Hillebrand, physician to the royal family, established
the garden in 1853. Hillebrand leased a small portion of land
from Queen Kalama, and he and his wife built a home on the
upper terrace, which was constructed of lava stones. Hillebrand,
author of *Flora of the Hawaiian Islands* (1886), introduced more
than 160 species of plants, some (like the Java plum) that he collected during a tour of the tropical Orient. After he returned to
Europe in 1871, the property was sold to Captain Thomas Foster
and his wife Mary, who continued to develop the garden. Upon
Mary Foster's death in 1930, the five-and-a-half-acre site was
given to Honolulu County, which opened the botanical garden
in 1931. Over the next 27 years, Dr. Harold L. Lyon, the garden's
first director, introduced 10,000 new kinds of trees and plants,
including species and primary hybrid orchids from his own collection that are displayed in the Lyon wild orchid garden. The
Foster Garden was later expanded to 14 acres from the late
1950s to 1989. It is one of five gardens that comprise the
Honolulu Botanical Gardens and is listed on the National

Register of Historic Places. Many of its subtropical plants are now nearly 150 years old,
including the magnificent specimens that
tower over the upper terrace—the two great
Kapok trees, the Queensland Kauri tree, a
broadleaf conifer, and the elephant earpod
tree, so named for its ear-shaped seed pod.
In the nineteenth century, these trees were
prized for shipbuilding purposes such as
providing sturdy masts and cordage. They
are among 26 "exceptional" trees in the garden noted for their age, rarity, and beauty.
Another is the Bo tree, sacred to Buddhists,
and propagated from a famous Sri Lankan
Bo tree brought from India in the 3rd century B.C. An African Baobab tree has a 30-
foot girth. A rare double coconut palm from
the Seychelles Islands has the largest and
heaviest seeds of any plant—nuts weigh up
to 50 pounds. Other special collections
include palms, bromeliads, heliconias, gingers, and the prehistoric glen, which has
ancient "dinosaur" plants, such as cycads
dating to the Jurassic period.

9 Oahu: Lili`uokalani Botanical Garden

LOCATION: IN DOWNTOWN HONOLULU, JUST NORTH OF FOSTER GARDEN,
BETWEEN NORTH KUAKINI AND SCHOOL STREETS

GARDEN OPEN: 9am–4pm
daily, closed New Year's Day
and Christmas Day

ADMISSION: Free

FURTHER INFORMATION FROM:
Department of Parks and
Recreation
50 North Vineyard Boulevard
Honolulu, Oahu 96817.
808.522.7066

The Lili`uokalani Botanical Garden displays native Hawaiian plants. In contrast to the Foster Botanical Garden (to which it is connected via an underpass beneath the H-1 Freeway) this garden shows the landscape before Westerners settled Hawaii in the nineteenth century. One of Honolulu's five publicly owned botanical gardens, this seven-and-a-half-acre urban park was separated from the Foster Garden when the freeway was built. It was once the property and favorite picnic grounds of Queen Lili`uokalani, the last reigning monarch of Hawaii, who gifted it to Honolulu in 1908 to be used as a public park. Exotic trees were cleared out for a recent renovation, and the monkeypod trees that the Queen planted along the Nu`uanu stream were retained. More than 40 native plant species were added, such as *loulu* (Hawaiian palm), *wiliwili* (coral tree), Hawaiian poppies, and *ma`o hau hele*, or yellow hibiscus, the endangered state flower. Waikahalulu Falls, which cascades over worn lava rocks into a swimming pool below, has been a favorite place to play for generations of local children. With a lawn, picnic tables, and benches, the garden offers a relaxing place to enjoy a small piece of the native Hawaiian landscape in the midst of the city.

OPPOSITE, TOP: *Couroupita guianensis*
OPPOSITE, BOTTOM: *Orchid Garden at Foster Botanical Garden*
BELOW: *Sunrise on Koolau*

GARDEN OPEN: 9am–4pm daily; closed New Year's Day and Christmas Day
ADMISSION: Free
FURTHER INFORMATION FROM: 1396 California Avenue Wahiawa, Oahu 96786. 808.621.7321

10 Oahu: Wahiawa Botanic Garden

LOCATION: ON CALIFORNIA AVENUE, OFF KAMEHAMEHA HIGHWAY H-2

Cradled between the Waianae and Koolau mountain ranges in central Oahu, the Wahiawa Botanic Garden was used in the 1920s by the Hawaii Sugar Planters' Association for forestry experiments and as a nursery for plants that thrive in cool, humid areas. Given to the city of Honolulu in 1950, this model rain forest garden is known as the "tropical jewel" of the five Honolulu Botanical Gardens. A self-guided brochure directs visitors through the 27-acre garden and forested ravine. A path from the entrance leads past mulesfoot and Australian tree ferns to the upper terrace, planted with trees such as Indian mahogany and red river trees, allspice, and Chinese cinnamon and camphor trees. Other paths wind through collections of aroids, gingers, heliconias, and palms. Be sure to look up into the trees, for this garden specializes in ephiphytes—plants whose roots need air rather than soil—including some unusual ferns, orchids, and cacti that cling to the trees. The garden also features native plants such as *hapu'u*, or Hawaiian tree ferns, whose soft yellowish-brown wool (*pulu*) Hawaiians used as a dressing for wounds and in embalming the dead. Other natives include *loulu* palms, Hawaiian hibiscus, and *'ie'ie*, a vine whose long aerial roots were used to make baskets and fish traps and which is considered sacred to Laka, Goddess of the Hula.

GARDEN OPEN: 10am–5:30pm daily
ADMISSION: Entrance into park is $24 plus tax for adults, $12 plus tax ages 4-12, and free for children under 3
FURTHER INFORMATION FROM: Waimea Arboretum Foundation 59-864 Kamehameha Highway Haleiwa, Oahu 96712. 808.638.8655

11 Oahu: Waimea Arboretum and Botanical Gardens

LOCATION: WITHIN WAIMEA VALLEY ADVENTURE PARK, ON THE NORTH SHORE ABOUT 5 MILES NORTH OF HALEIWA

The Waimea Arboretum and Botanical Gardens encompasses a serene 150 acres within the 1,800-acre Waimea Valley Adventure Park, which offers such activities as mountain biking and kayaking. (A $25 donation to the Waimea Arboretum Foundation entitles visitors to park admission for a year, as well as discounts within the park at the store and for food and beverages.) The arboretum and botanical gardens display 6,000 different types of plants in 35 distinct gardens organized by geography, plant families, and special uses. Their focus is on rare and endangered species, and you will see plants here that you might not see elsewhere, such as *Kokia cookei*, a Hawaiian mallow that is extinct in the wild. The plants are labeled; those that are endangered are identified with red labels. The garden grows rare heritage plants for the Center for Plant Conservation, and exchanges seeds and plant materials with

other botanical institutions and researchers worldwide. Among
the threatened flora cultivated here are species from several
island groups such as the Marianas and the Mascarenes. Two
miles of paths and asphalt roads lead past four ponds, a 45-foot
waterfall, and through gardens that feature native Hawaiian
plants, including hibiscus and heirloom crops. You can wander
through horticultural history in the hibiscus evolution garden
and view more than 85 of the world's 112 species of red and
orange-flowering coral trees (*Erythrina*), perhaps the world's
largest collection. Other special collections include a palm
meadow, bamboo, mallows, ferns, plants of Central and South
America, tropical fruits, and beautiful flowering collections of
gingers, heliconias, and flowers used in ancient and modern
times for leis.

*The bromeliad collection at
Waimea*

159

GARDEN OPEN: Guided walking tours Monday through Friday, by reservation only; call for specific tour times
ADMISSION: $10 for adults; children 12 and younger free
FURTHER INFORMATION FROM:
P.O. Box 95
Hana, Maui 96713.
808.248.8912
www.ntbg.org

12 Maui: Kahanu Garden

LOCATION: BETWEEN HANA AIRPORT AND HANA TOWN, ON HANA HIGHWAY

The Kahanu Garden grows amid black lava flows in the splendid isolation of Maui's rugged far eastern shores. Located on cliffs over the coast with spectacular views of the Pacific to the east and Mount Haleakala to the west the garden specializes in the collection and study of plants significant to the Hawaiian and Polynesian cultures. It is also the site of the *Pi`ilanihale Heiau,* an ancient Hawaiian temple built of tiers of lava stones, and the sixteenth-century residence of Maui's revered King Pi`ilani. In the king's time, the region was an important agricultural area with its abundant rainfall and rich earth. After Westerners arrived in the mid-1800s, this fertile alluvial land was converted into sugarcane fields, and in 1946 became cattle pastures for the Hana Ranch. The *heiau* was designated a National Historic Landmark in 1964. The owners of the property, the Kananu-Matsuda family and the Hana Ranch, eventually began to search for a way to preserve this sacred site, and in 1972 granted 61 acres of land surrounding the *heiau* to the National Tropical Botanical Garden. The NTBG later acquired an adjoining 62 acres of land and expanded the garden.
Fringed by a vast native forest of screwpines (*Pandanus*), whose leaves are used for thatch and baskets, Kahanu Garden has the world's largest collection of `ulu, or breadfruit. More than 120 cultivars of this plant are being grown and studied as a source of wood, fiber, medicines, and adhesives, and food (its nutritious fruit was a traditional staple of the Hawaiian diet). The garden also grows extensive collections of plants such as native *Pritchardia* palms, coconuts, bananas, vanilla, and `awa (kava). Though Kahanu Garden may not look like a formal or landscape garden in its design, it offers a fascinating glimpse into the life and culture of ancient Hawaii.

GARDEN OPEN: 9am–4pm daily
ADMISSION: $5 adults, $1 children ages 6-12
FURTHER INFORMATION FROM:
R.R. 4, Box 288
Kula, Maui 96790.
808.878.1715

13 Maui: Kula Botanical Garden

LOCATION: ON KEKAULIKE AVENUE/HIGHWAY 377, JUST UNDER A MILE FROM KULA HIGHWAY

Embraced by the gorges of two streambeds on the slopes of Haleakala Crater, the Kula Botanical Gardens enjoy a luxuriant and relaxing natural setting. At 3,300 feet in elevation, the garden has cool nights and wonderful views of the West Maui Mountains and Maalaea and Kahului Bays (from the gazebo, the entire length of the Central Valley is visible, from sea level to 10,221 feet in elevation). Off in the distance are the islands of Lanai and Molokai. The six-acre garden is the work of Warren

McCord, a landscape architect, and his wife Helen, who moved to Maui and bought this land in 1969. In the beginning, they had to clear the land of wattle, or acacia, a weedy tree introduced from Australia that had overtaken the native plants. They then began planting trees and tropical and semi-tropical plants, and opened the garden to the public in 1971. An easy walk takes you through the garden on wheelchair-accessible paths. The garden's 1,500+ plant varieties include over 40 different kinds of proteas, beautiful exotic shrubs with cone-like flowerheads that make exquisite and hardy cut flowers. Originally from South Africa and Australia, proteas were introduced to Hawaii in the early 1970s, but grow only in a few places on the islands because they prefer cooler air (the garden sells protea seeds so you may attempt growing them at home). Throughout the garden are fruit and nut trees such mango, persimmon, avocado, strawberry guava, macadamia, and candlenut (*kukui*) trees. Jacaranda trees show off lavender blossoms from February through November. The garden's cool mountain air allows for trees that are usually not found in Hawaii: deciduous maples, crape myrtles, and Monterey pines grown to be sold as Christmas trees. The garden also features a large fern collection with native Hawaiian tree ferns and Haleakala ferns, as well as day lilies and small orange and red epidendrum orchids that offer brilliant contrasts to the various greens of tropical foliage and dark hues of volcanic rock. Other special collections are displayed within the orchid house, the bromeliad house, and the fuchsia house. The garden's aviary is home to Java rice birds, blue pheasant, African heron, and love birds. With features that imitate nature, such as a stream with waterfalls that empty into a koi pond, the garden also draws wild birds such as Japanese white eyes and Hawaiian apapanis.

TOP: *A shady outpost at Kula Botanical Garden*
BOTTOM: *Kula Botanical Garden's koi pond invites wild birds like Hawaiian apapanis.*

14 Hawaii: Hawaii Tropical Botanical Garden

LOCATION: SEVEN MILES NORTHEAST OF HILO, ON THE 4 MILE SCENIC ROUTE ALONG THE HAMAKUA COAST

In Hawaiian, *onomea* means "the best place," and the Hawaii Tropical Botanical Garden's location in the sheltered Onomea Valley embodies this ideal. Protected from buffeting tradewinds and blessed with rich volcanic soil, an international collection of more than 3,000 tropical plant species flourishes on the rocky Hamakua coast. The nonprofit garden's mission is to be a sanctuary for rain forest plants. It was created by a self-taught horticulturist, Dan J. Lutkenhouse, who grew fond of the Onomea Valley in 1977 while on vacation with his wife

GARDEN OPEN: 9am–4pm daily (gate closes at 5pm); closed New Year's Day, Thanksgiving and Christmas Day
ADMISSION: $15 adult, $5 for ages 6-15
FURTHER INFORMATION FROM:
P.O. Box 80
Papaikou, Hawaii 96781.
808.964.5233
www.htbg.com

Pauline. He bought 17 acres of secluded coastline and devoted the next eight years to clearing the land of wild invasive trees, weeds, and thorn thickets that had taken over after the valley was deserted at the turn of the century. Lutkenhouse and his helpers cleared paths through the jungle following the contours of the land. During the process, he uncovered secrets such as a three-tiered waterfall and tall coconut palms, mango, and monkeypod trees planted up to 150 years ago, when the valley was a fishing village and later a port for shipping raw sugar produced at a mill some distance up the hill. Opened to the public in 1984, the garden follows a mile-long trail to the ocean through the original 17 acres (another 25 acres are as yet undeveloped). Along this trail are Amazon lilies, orchids, and a rare bat plant whose flowers open only for a day. Australian ironwood trees and majestic breadfruit trees flank the oceanfront trail. From Turtle Point, you can look down to a cove that is home to marine creatures such as *a'ama* crabs and, further out, sea turtles. The trail follows a stream through a palm forest and returns to Lily Lake. Here you'll find more than 100 species of tropical plants such as water hyacinths, giant Queen Victoria water lilies from Africa, and fan-shaped travelers trees from Madagascar. The bromeliad hill offers more than 80 kinds, including the variegated red pineapple. In the orchid garden, fragrant blooms of every hue are on exhibit, from white pha-

Some of the 80 species along the heliconia trail

laenopses to orange oncidiums. A small pond nearby is home to pink lesser flamingos and Mandarin ducks. A trail leads through a forest of torch gingers with tall, thick, red stalks and showy waxen red cones that bloom from May to July. At the heart of the garden is the giant fern circle, a primitive place formed by giant tree fern fronds, sword ferns, and cycads, descendants of the first plants colonized on the planet. The palm vista and palm jungle trails feature nearly 200 varieties—fishtail, sago, date, betel nut, the rare Peruvian *Euterpe precatoria*, and towering Alexandra palms that produce huge red seed clusters. Along the heliconia trail dangle the brilliant bracts of 80 different species, including the hanging lobster claw. In the banyan canyon, the multi-trunked tree shelters bamboo and a rare native Hawaiian gardenia known as *remyi*. Several side trails lead to vistas where you can contemplate the Onomea Stream and the waves crashing on lava rocks below.

15 Anchorage: Alaska Botanical Garden

LOCATION: ON CAMPBELL AIRSTRIP ROAD, NEXT TO BENNY BENSON SCHOOL AT CORNER OF TUDOR ROAD

Nestled in the foothills of the Chugach Mountains in a quiet area just east of Anchorage, the Alaska Botanical Garden celebrates native Alaskan plants and hardy introductions in a natural setting where Campbell Creek winds through a forest of birch and spruce. The garden contains more than 480 varieties of plants, including 92 native species. Trails wind through several themed gardens, such as a demonstration perennial garden with borders of birch logs and recycled concrete. The lower perennial garden displays hardy plants such as delphinium and bee balm. The rock garden, which is being developed by the Alaska Rock Garden Society, includes areas for both sun- and shade-loving plants. The herb garden is laid out in a classic design with four central raised beds and a latticework wall and arbor. Beyond the herb garden is the Lowenfels Family Nature Trail, a sweeping one-and-a-quarter-mile loop through a forest of alders, cottonwoods, black spruce, and birch, past bogs, meadows, and the creek. Just off the wildflower trail is a huge moss-covered boulder, the largest example of the garden's many glacial erratics, or stones and boulders deposited by glaci-

GARDEN OPEN: 9am–9pm daily

ADMISSION: By donation

FURTHER INFORMATION FROM: P.O. Box 202202 Anchorage 99520. 907.770.3692 http://www.alaska.net./ ~garden/

NEARBY SIGHTS OF INTEREST: Anchorage Museum of History and Art, Mann Leiser Memorial Greenhouse, Centennial Rose Garden at Delaney Park Strip

Colorful herb beds surrounded by the arbor

ers. Still under development, the botanic garden's 110 acres will include about 10 percent designed gardens and trails, while the remaining acreage will become a natural wildlife preserve. Because of the garden's proximity to the foothills' diverse fauna, you may see woodpeckers, lynx, moose, and bears, as well as king salmon spawning in the creek during the summer months. Opened to the public in 1993, the garden was ten years in the planning. In 1983, a committee of the Alaska Horticultural Association, including horticulturists, landscape architects, engineers, and local citizens, set out to establish a botanical garden for Alaska. Their research took them to more than 50 botanical gardens worldwide.In 1992, volunteers began building trails and planting the garden. The land is issued to the garden through a land-use agreement with the Municipality of Anchorage. Future plans include: a children's garden, a Japanese garden, a rose garden, and a visitors center. Today, though still under development, the garden gives a glimpse of the surprisingly diverse and rich array of plants that thrive in Alaska.

GARDEN OPEN: Dawn to dusk daily in summer

FURTHER INFORMATION FROM:
Chamber of Commerce
Visitors Center
P.O. Box 45
Palmer 99645.
907.745.2880

NEARBY SIGHTS OF INTEREST:
Our Colony House Museum, Musk Ox Farm, and Williams' Reindeer Farm

ABOVE: *A pebbly trail through the themed gardens at the Alaska Botanical Garden*

16 Palmer: Matanuska Valley Agricultural Showcase Garden

LOCATION: 45 MILES FROM ANCHORAGE, AT 723 SOUTH VALLEY WAY, AT CORNER ELMWOOD (NEXT TO THE PALMER VISITORS CENTER)

Garden lovers on their way from Anchorage to Denali National Park may wish to take a detour to Palmer to stroll through the Matanuska Valley Agricultural Showcase Garden. Here you'll find thematic garden beds filled with annuals, perennials, vegetables, herbs, and fruits, as well as plants for special uses such as windbreaks and revegetation. The garden was created in 1988 by local horticulturist Wendy Anderson. The quarter-acre, intensively cultivated garden features demonstration areas of soil-warming techniques (using plastic tunnels and heat-retaining cloth) and gardening for small spaces. A colonist's garden of vegetables and flowers available in the region back in the pioneer days of the 1930s greets visitors outside the entrance to the garden, which is flanked by *Clematis tangutica*. Circular beds in

the center are filled with herbs and edible flowers. In the northeast quadrant are a cottage-garden border of annual and perennial flowers and an "everlasting garden" of flowers, seed pods,
and leaves that can be cut and dried. Along the eastern edge is a
windbreak of willows, elderberry, cotoneaster, spirea, and evergreens. Native plants that can be used as ground covers and for
perennial borders fill the southeast corner. Nearby are a rock
garden and beds of commercial crops grown in the Matanuska
Valley, such as potatoes, lettuces, and enormous O.S. Cross cab-
bage. Along the south and west perimeters are raspberries,
gooseberries, currants, and other small fruits. These lush gardens are all the more fantastic when you consider the region
once (18,000 years ago) was covered by the Matanuska Glacier.
Though it has receded from this part of the valley, the glacier
still looms at the mouth of the Matanuska River, spanning 27
miles in length and four miles in width (the icy mass is best
seen from the Glenn Highway north of Palmer).

BELOW: *Vegetable plots and
flower beds at the University
of Alaska's Georgeson
Botanical Garden*

17 Fairbanks: The Georgeson Botanical Garden

LOCATION: WEST TANANA DRIVE ON THE UNIVERSITY OF ALASKA FAIRBANKS
CAMPUS

The Georgeson Botanical Garden continues a tradition that
began during the gold rush era. In 1905, the citizens of the
Fairbanks area petitioned the Secretary of Agriculture to establish an experiment station in the Tanana Valley. Alaska agricultural pioneer Charles Georgeson, director of the Alaska
Agricultural Experiment Stations, selected 1,394 acres in the
fertile valley, which at the time contained 82 homesteads. From
the start, the station focused on cultivating grains, grasses, and
potatoes, but always had plots of vegetables, flowers, fruits, and
ornamental plants. In the 1970s, the garden area was expanded
to include colorful demonstration flower beds, and in the

GARDEN OPEN: Dawn to dusk
in summer
ADMISSION: $1 donation
TOURS: Free guided tours 2
pm Friday, June through
August; group tours by reser-
vation, $2 per person, $25
minimum
FURTHER INFORMATION FROM:
Box 757200
University of Alaska
Fairbanks 99775.
907.474.5651
www.lter.uaf.edu/~salrm/GRB

1980s, it became a botanical garden. Today, researchers at the three-acre garden study the propagation, cultivation, and conservation of native and introduced plant species in the sub-arctic north. About 1,000 plants are studied each year, including new varieties of annual and perennial flowers, shrubs, vegetables from artichokes to zucchini (including 50-pound cabbages), and fruits such as raspberries. A perennial garden features hardy shrub roses, peonies, day lilies, and iris, including a native wild iris that ranges in color from white to burgundy. Nearly 300 kinds of annual flowers are tested, including many that—because of the amount of sunlight they receive—are easily twice the size of flowers in the "Lower 48" (pansies, for example, have enormous "faces" on 18-inch stalks). There is a water garden, a children's pond garden, and an area of hardy ferns. An herb garden of medicinal plants used by the Athabaskan Indians is being created, and future collections will include more ornamental plants and a garden of native wildflowers. The garden is part of the 1,000-acre Agricultural and Forestry Experiment Station, which also includes a farm with animals such as pigs, cows, and reindeer. Also on this land is the Smith Lake Boreal Arboretum, accessed by 26 miles of hiking and Nordic ski trails. The trails wind through a mixed birch and white spruce forest where native plants are labeled. The lake is a bird and birders' haven, with sandhill cranes, ducks, hawks, and the occasional golden eagle.

Ornamental and native wild flowers at Georgeson Botanical Garden

Index

University of California Botanical
    Garden, *40, 53–54*
University of Hawaii, 154
University of Idaho Arboretum and
    Botanical Garden, *viii*, 19,
    20–21
University of Southern California, 88
University of Utah, 16
University of Washington, 123, 130,
    132
Utah, *viii*, 2, 16–19

V
Vail, Colorado, *viii*, 1–2, 11
Vilett, Helene, 54
Villa Montalvo, *40*, 68–69
Villa Pisani (Italy), as model, 75
Virginia Robinson Gardens, *40*, 74–75

W
W. D. Holley Plant Environmental
    Research Center, *viii*, 3
W. W. Seymour Botanical
    Conservatory, *100*, 138–39
Wagner, Corydon, 102, 140–41
Wagner, Eulalie, 102, 140–41

Wahiawa Botanic Garden, *142*, 158
Waimea Arboretum and Botanical
    Gardens, *142*, 158
Waimea Arboretum Foundation, 158
Waimea Valley, 158
Walker, Dr. Milton, 136
Walker, Hal, 95
Walnut Creek, California, *40*, 59
Walska, Mme. Ganna. *See* Ganna
    Walska Lotusland
Washington Park Arboretum, *100*,
    130–31
Washington (state), *100*–2, 122–41
Washington State Centennial, 136
Webster, Gertrude Divine, 25
Wenatchee, Washington, *100*, 102, 133
Weyerhaeuser Company, 136
Wheelwright, George, 45
White, George, 95
Wichman, Charles "Chipper," 145–46
Wichman, Juliet Rice, 145
Wilbur D. May Arboretum &
    Botanical Garden, *40*, 42, 97
Willamette River, 107–8, 117, 119
Willard, Stephen, 89
Wilson, Jean, 30–31

Wilson, Richard, 30–31
Witt, J. A. *See* Washington Park
    Arboretum
Woodland Park Rose Garden, *100, 128*
Woodside, California, *40*–41, 63
Worn, Annie, 46
Worn, George A., 46
Worn, Isabella, 63
Wyoming, *viii*, 2, 15

X
Xeriscape Demonstration Garden,
    viii, 1–2, *13–14*

Y
Yoch, Florence, 86
Young, Brigham, 19

Z
Zen Center. *See* San Francisco Zen
    Center
Zumwalt, Rex, 137

173

Acknowledgments

I'd like to thank all my family and friends whose enthusiasm and encouragement allowed me to research and write this book. My gratitude and love go especially to my parents, Joanne and David, without whom I could not have completed this project, my sister Angela, and my dear friend Barb. I thank Eugenia Bell, my editor, for all her diplomatic help. My appreciation, also to the gardens who contributed their photos to the book.

The Golden Age of American Gardens by Mac Griswold and Eleanor Weller provided valuable insight into some of the historic gardens in this book.

I dedicate this book to my husband, Michael, and our children, Nora and Vito, whose love, humor, and appreciation for the natural world have provided immeasurable inspiration and support.

Photograph credits

Kit Amorn © The Huntington Library: 80 (middle and top)
R. Baker: 154
John Blades: 71, cover
Jim Bones: 45
Richard A. Brown: 100, 122, 124 (top and bottom), 125 (top and bottom)
Robert Burroughs: 96
Claire Curran: 77
Don El-Monte: 85
Nicki Foster: 155
Jacqueline Gaer: 46
A.H. Guhl: 32
Steve Gunther: 95
David Hancocks: 33
Will Hart: 97
Havey Productions: 4 (bottom), 6 (top and bottom), 7 (top and bottom)
Mel Lewis: xvi, 17
Christine Mather: 34
Stephen McCabe: 70 (top)

Kathleen McCormick: 2, 12, 14, 22, 25, 26, 27 (top and bottom), 28, 29, 31 (top and bottom), 49, 52 , 53, 54, 55, 57, 60, 62, 64, 65, 66, 67, 69, 104, 105, 108, 111, 115, 112, 115, 116, 117, 126, 127, 128, 129, 132, 135, 138, 140, 141, 145, 146, 147, 148 (bottom), 150, 151, 162, 175
R.J. Naskali: 20
Diane Ronayne: 21
San Francisco Recreation and Park Department: 50 (top)
Bob Schlosser © The Huntington Library: 78 (bottom)
Lennie Siegel: 44
Joy Spurs: 130
Michael R. Stoklos: 24

All other photos appear courtesy of the respective gardens